w h y
it's hard
to love
j e s u s

why
it's hard
to love
Jesus

JOSEPH M. STOWELL

MOODY PUBLISHERS
CHICAGO

© 2003 by
JOSEPH M. STOWELL

Originally published as
Loving Christ: Recapturing Your Passion for Jesus
© 2000 by Joseph M. Stowell
Zondervan Publishing House

All Scripture quotations, unless otherwise indicated, are taken from the *Holy Bible, New International Version*®. NIV®. Copyright © 1973, 1978, 1984 by International Bible Society. Used by permission of Zondervan Publishing House. All rights reserved.

Library of Congress Cataloging-in-Publication Data

Stowell, Joseph M.
   [Loving Christ]
   Why it's hard to love Jesus / Joseph M.Stowell.
     p. cm.
   Originally published: Loving Christ. Grand Rapids, MI : Zondervan Publishing House, © 2000.
   Includes bibliographical references.
   ISBN 0-8024-1092-8
   1. Love--Religious aspects--Christianity. I. Title.

BV4639.S76 2003
241'.4--dc21

2003007136

1 3 5 7 9 10 8 6 4 2

Printed in the United States of America

To the students at Moody Bible Institute,
whose fresh and energetic love for Jesus
inspires and refreshes my desire
to love Him more

contents

with
Thanks . . .

I f your life is impacted by this book, then please thank . . .

Jesus, without whose matchless love none of us could enjoy the privilege of a loving relationship with Him.

Martie, my wife, whose interest in seeing this message make it into your hands and ultimately into your heart meant she endured the hardships of being a "book widow" as I got lost in the process of writing.

My friends at Moody Publishers, who captured a

vision for the project and made an enthusiastic commitment to bring it to you.

Jack Kuhatschek, for mentoring me in my writing and helping to organize the thoughts and concepts in ways that more effectively communicate.

Lori Imhof, whose service to my ministry as executive secretary helped keep the decks clear so I had time to write.

preface

Several years ago, I had occasion to enjoy a concert by the Brooklyn Tabernacle Choir singing in Chicago. Without question, the message that came through loud and clear was that what they were presenting was much more than a mere performance. They skillfully and beautifully interspersed moving, heartfelt testimony with powerful musical selections, giving clear witness to the fact that so many in the choir had been redeemed from the pit and rubble of sin and pain rampant in that part of Brooklyn, New York.

One song in particular captured my attention: "I'm Not Afraid Anymore." The powerful lyrics penetrated my heart. There I sat, the busy bee for Jesus, comfortable in my pin-striped suit, neatly pressed and color-coordinated. For most of us who live in safe environments, it is hard to identify with the lyrics, but they were being sung on that Saturday afternoon by people who used to live in constant fear: fear of violence, fear of not having enough money, fear of what might happen to their children, fear of not being able to get the drugs needed to feed their addictions, fear of every to-morrow. As the soloist sang the powerful words, the spot-lights showed glistening tears trickling down his cheeks. Later I learned why he wept as he sang.

The singer's name is Calvin Hunt. Although he was mar-ried and had several children, his family life had been less than ideal. He had gotten really messed up with crack co-caine, and eventually hit bottom. For years he frequented crack dens and dark places riddled with crime and all man-ner of sexual deviations.

Remarkably, through the witness of his young daughter, Calvin surrendered everything to Christ and his life has never been the same. He had been in the pits of hell, and by God's grace he found a path to heaven.

Today Calvin sings of not being afraid anymore and stirs thousands each year singing songs such as "Mercy Saw Me" and "I'm Clean." And every time he sings you get the dis-tinct impression that these songs come from the heart of one who has been forgiven much.

In a strange, honest way, I confess I sat envious of that sort of emotional, grace-born attachment to the Savior. To feel, and more important, to undestand what it meant to be among "the forgiven-much." But I was forced by it all to ask myself, "Do I love Jesus that way?"

If Jesus asked you if you loved Him, how would you answer? No doubt you'd respond quickly like Peter, "Of course I love You!" But what if He persisted and asked again, "Do you love Me?" Would that strike you as odd? Would you be confused or put out? Jesus asked Peter that penetrating question three times before Peter's insistence seemed to satisfy Him. Jesus knew that words alone could not accurately measure the depth of Peter's affection. And that goes for you and me. Christ desires that our devotion to Him run deeper than just our words. Ultimately, He wants us to demonstrate that love in how we live. Loving Him is not a throwaway issue to be done or not to be done at our own pleasure. In fact, our joy and effectiveness as a follower of Jesus rises or falls on living out a genuine love for Him.

Don't we grow accustomed to this profound and humbling reality? The almighty God of the universe longs to have a deep, abiding, love-filled relationship with you. We are not simply trophies of grace that line the shelves of His throne room. You are treasured by Him and He right now is waiting for you to return the favor of the expansive love that He has showered on you. This kind of a relationship only grows out of a deep awareness of our need for grace and the One who freely gives it. Without this gripping soul dynamic of knowing that we are among the "forgiven-much," it will be hard to really love Jesus. Genuine, grace-born love for Christ is rare. Too often we live out our faith in the burdensome and boring world of duty and habit. Choked by busy lives and creature comforts, it is easy for us to let the glowing embers of a once vibrant love slowly dwindle, leaving us with a barren religious routine that is loveless and mundane.

Why It's Hard to Love Jesus is about moving from faith expressed in empty ritual to a dynamic, love-filled devotion lived out in a deepening relationship with Jesus. It's about confronting the Pharisee in all of us and embracing a genuine love for Christ. To get there we must first look at a story . . . an ancient narrative about two individuals, plucked from obscurity by Luke, the master storyteller. First is Simon the Pharisee, the "good guy" known for his clean record and pristine religion—both of which he gladly keeps on full display. The second is an unnamed commoner, whose only distinction was that she was "a woman who had lived a sinful life."

Both encounter Jesus. And in their varied responses, they provide compelling portraits of what it means to love Jesus and why it is often hard for those of us who live "good" lives to love Him authentically. Our challenge in this adventure to capture a vibrant love for Jesus will be whether or not we can be honest enough to admit that we tend to be far more like the loveless Simon than the sinning woman.

An Encounter with Jesus

*Now one of the Pharisees invited Jesus to have dinner with him,
so he went to the Pharisee's house and reclined at the table.
When a woman who had lived a sinful life in that town learned
that Jesus was eating at the Pharisee's house, she brought an alabaster jar of perfume, and as she stood behind him at his feet
weeping, she began to wet his feet with her tears. Then she wiped
them with her hair, kissed them and poured perfume on them.*

*When the Pharisee who had invited him saw this, he said to him-
self, "If this man were a prophet, he would know who is touching
him and what kind of woman she is—that she is a sinner."*

*Then [Jesus] turned toward the woman and said to Simon, "Do
you see this woman? I came into your house. You did not give me
any water for my feet, but she wet my feet with her tears and
wiped them with her hair. You did not give me a kiss, but this
woman, from the time I entered, has not stopped kissing my feet.
You did not put oil on my head, but she has poured perfume on my
feet. Therefore, I tell you, her many sins have been forgiven—for
she loved much. But he who has been forgiven little loves little."*

Then Jesus said to her, "Your sins are forgiven."
—Luke 7:36–39, 44–48

Chapter One

The Eclipse of Devotion

THE PHARISEE IN ALL OF US

Wᵉ all have a love language. For some it's touch; for others, it's affirming words or generous acts of kindness. Early in our marriage I learned Martie's love language.

When I got married I believed flowers were love's universal language. So one evening I did the old dozen-roses-behind-my-back, kiss-on-the-cheek routine, fully believing Martie would swoon in my arms. She graciously thanked me, sniffed them, smiled, and took them to the kitchen.

Not exactly the response I had expected. I followed her into the kitchen and asked if the flowers were a disappointment. She said she liked them a lot, but wondered how much money they had cost. I was a seminary student and money was tight. As I recall, the flowers cost more than the monthly rent. Understandably, for Martie, the flowers had only compounded our financial woes. For me they were a message of love.

> SEEKING THE APPROVAL OF OTHERS ALWAYS LEADS US AWAY FROM WHAT MATTERS.

The flowers didn't connect. My assumptions and Martie's expectations were miles apart. My time and attention make her feel most loved. When I pay close attention to Martie she's convinced how much I value her. Joining her and affirming her in her world says "I love you" in far deeper tones than flowers.

Jesus has a love language. The Bible provides several examples of the authentic love that touches His heart. Scripture also shows many people who thought they loved Him but missed the mark. The compelling story in Luke 7 includes both. See if you can find yourself in the story.

LIVING LIFE LOVELESSLY

Like my misguided attempts to show Martie my love, our goodness, busyness for Christ, and conformity to rules of behavior may not connect with Jesus. Simon the Pharisee would have proudly proclaimed that he loved God. He followed the codes and traditions of the Law and lived a respectable life. He piously viewed the woman's shocking invasion of the dinner party as rude and repulsive. Her sinning way, in his mind, had put her far from the touch and love of God. Yet Jesus endorsed her love. But surprisingly, Simon's approach to pleasing God didn't connect with Christ.

That's the major lesson from Luke's story. It doesn't matter if we think that we love Him. What matters is whether or not Christ feels loved by us.

Simon failed the test. Blinded by false perceptions, he couldn't see how far from God he really lived.

Now that's convicting! I'll be honest; life in the religious limelight is laden with land mines. I struggle every day to keep my focus on Christ. Deep down, I love the approving nods from board members, faculty, and students. After all, they're looking to me for leadership—for a model of genuine faithfulness. But that's a land mine. Seeking the approval of others always leads us away from what matters. Jesus wants my heart. He's most concerned about my relationship to Him.

> CHRISTIANITY IS NOT JUST ABOUT WHAT WE ARE ARE DOING; IT IS FIRST AND FOREMOST ABOUT WHAT HE HAS DONE FOR US.

Anyone who assumes that Christianity is about garnering applause for good behavior has only to read Revelation 2:2–5. It shatters the notion that busyness and behavioral conformity are the same as loving Christ. Through the apostle John, Jesus spoke to the believers at Ephesus, say-ing, "I know your deeds, your hard work and your perse-verance. I know that you cannot tolerate wicked men, that you have tested those who claim to be apostles but are not, and have found them false. You have persevered and have endured hardships for my name, and have not grown weary." What a list of compliments. Sounds like a great bunch of folks—mature, wise, faithful to the truth. I know of countless Christians who'd long to have such a glowing assessment of their lives. But that's not all Christ had to say. He continued, "Yet I hold this against you: You have for-saken your first love."

The church at Ephesus had been doing all the right things. And although Jesus acknowledged that, He had a deeper concern. They didn't love Him like they used to love Him. Their passion had been eclipsed by the routine and rit-ual of good behavior and faithful religious responses. Jesus reproved them because their love for Christ was not their chief priority. Put another way, they did what they did for all the wrong reasons. Perhaps their good behavior was spurred by a sense of religious obligation. Or they may have tried to live up to the expectations of others. Their obedience may have been driven by the fear of consequences. They may have given because they thought they would be blessed in return. And they may have thought it their duty to defend the faith against false prophets. But it wasn't enough.

THE TROUBLE WITH A DUTIFUL LIFE

There is a well-traveled detour on the way to heaven—a worn path that leads to a dead-end street of good works for good works sake.

Oswald Chambers writes:

We consider what we do in the way of Christian work as service, yet Jesus Christ calls service to be what we are to Him, not what we do for Him. Discipleship is based solely on devotion to Jesus Christ. . . . Today we have substituted doctrinal belief for personal belief, and that is why so many people are devoted to causes and so few are devoted to Jesus Christ.[1]

Christianity is not just about what we are doing; it is first and foremost about what *He has done for us.* It is not just about what we are becoming; it is about what He has become for us. As a result, all our good works and all our service to Him are not obligations, but rather opportunities for us to express our love and gratitude for all the greatness of His grace toward us. Doing all we do as a response rather than a ritual is the heart of Jesus' love language.

When we obey all the rules and perform dutifully for the world to see, pride creeps in and takes hold. But it is not just pride that snares us. When our Christianity is primarily about duty and doing, we eventually become tired of being good for the sake of being good. Christianity not practiced out of loving gratitude for Christ grows dull and unattentive.

As one observer notes, a believer caught in this trap becomes,

humorless, prudish, constrained in his affections, incapable of enjoying himself, repressed, inhibited, pouting and censorious.
    There are hundreds of people like that today: respect-
.able, conventional, good people. They look down their noses at the permissive society; they curl their lip at the decay in moral standards. They think they're good, but they are not;

they're simply dull. They think they're being moral, but they are not; they're simply feeling sanctimonious.

Joyless in their hypocrisy, sterile in their respectability, their religion has no more in common with Christianity than a frigid marriage has in common with a real love affair.[2]

Those words sting, but they're true. I recall asking a student at Moody about her boyfriend. She simply said, "He adores me!" I love the response. We have to ask if that is how Christ feels about our love for Him.

True Christianity is always about the One who has loved us and given Himself for us. When we drift from this motivation and begin to be good because we are Christians, we elevate self above the Savior. When that happens, the door swings open to arrogance and self-righteousness. What occurs is an eclipse of devotion.

Simon's pharisaical approach to faith had eclipsed what mattered most—that he be rightly related to Jesus.

THE PHARISEE IN ALL OF US

The Pharisees were a society of pious men zealous for keeping the Law. Their name originates from an Aramaic root word that means "separate and distinct." That separateness marked them in society. They were not only Law keepers but also Law interpreters. They were "good works" police, so to speak.

The Pharisees did not start out as bad guys. They were motivated by a genuine desire to please God. But they deceived themselves into thinking that a human-centered religion would satisfy the divine requirement. That explains their vehement disdain for sinners. Sinners were second only to tax collectors in their judgment. They would never qualify to live among their ranks—they were permanent outcasts from God's society of the redeemed.

That same trap is laid for all of us. The only way to avoid being ensnared is to be aware of the lies that draw us in. There are at least four traps of Pharisaism that threaten our love for Jesus.

1. *The better we become, the more impressed we are with ourselves.* Jesus noted that the Pharisees enjoyed praying in public and went to great lengths to ensure that people knew they were fasting. They threw their money noisily into large trumpet-shaped depositories at the temple door for the world to see. They were guilty of self-focused devotion.

We are all vulnerable to be snagged in the same trap. After a series of sermons on being a servant, I decided to practice what I preached by pouring coffee for each of the deacons at the church board meeting. As I "served," one of them remarked, "Look, our pastor has a servant's heart!" I loved the sound of that! I poured coffee again at the next meeting, but now for a different reason. In the darkest corners of my heart I hoped people would notice my "servant's heart."

A parent of a student wrote and said how much her daughter was getting out of her experience, and that she appreciated my humility. As I read the letter, that particular part had a nice ring to it. In fact, I kind of enjoy writing about it now!

It is hard to love Jesus when we love ourselves more. As Shakespeare said, "There's the rub!" We start out doing what we do as an act of loving Him and end up loving ourselves.

2. *The better we become, the greater distance we place between ourselves and those we consider not as good.* The

infamous prayer of the Pharisees, "Lord, I thank you that I am not like . . . ," reflects the proud distance they maintained from the less righteous among them. It never occurred to them that we are all beggars telling other beggars where to find bread. Regardless of how we try to cover ourselves, most of us feel that we really are better than those who "live in sin." But we are not better—not at all. We are forgiven but not better. That sort of high-minded thinking leads us to become sanctimonious, judgmental, uncompassionate, and disinterested in the welfare of unbelievers.

Lisa DePalma is a graduate of Moody. God gave her a burden for the female prostitutes of Chicago. On Friday and Saturday nights she spends time on the streets with a ministry companion telling these sin-laden girls about Christ's liberating love. Always used and never loved, they hear—some of them for the first time—how God has wonderfully loved them in Jesus Christ.

But most of us think of street women as "wasted lives" beyond the pull of God's grace.

But aren't you and I just as hopeless as they are without the love of Christ? Of course we are. That reality should make our souls shudder. Imagine where you might be today if it were not for His grace! Jesus once welcomed you into His family, and He welcomes them too.

3. *The better we feel we are becoming, the more godless we may be.* The Pharisees became so fond of being good that they kept inventing new traditions and codes to obey. In the process they became stricter than God. In fact, Jesus reproved them for placing spiritual burdens on people that God never intended. Godliness means to be like God. Any addition to or subtraction from who He is, what He is like, and what He

requires is a move away from Him. Ungodliness is not always about the really bad people. Sometimes it is about the really good people who are more restrictive than God.

The Pharisees' good intentions led them astray. They took the laws of God and added extra rules for good measure. These were called "fence laws." Since women were viewed as a source of temptation and moral failure, the Pharisees prohibited rabbis from talking to a woman. They could not even walk along the same side of the street as a woman. Eventually, the fence laws came to hold an equal place with God's Laws. There were fence laws about the Sabbath, about purity, and about anything that had to do with righteous living. That's why Jesus was such a menace to the Pharisees. He insisted on tearing down those carefully constructed fences.

Those who lived through the sixties recall the hippie subculture in the United States. That time in American history represents the antithesis of all that believers hold sacred. Morality, purity in marriage, the dignity of the body, and respect for authority were ridiculed. Hippies advocated free love and communal living. Drugs released them from the constraints of authority. Rebellion against all that was proper and "straight" was the theme of the day.

So Christians reacted by enacting their own set of fence laws. Short hair and shaven faces for men became marks of spirituality. Dresses and no denim for women. Strict standards for choir and platform personnel. New rules in college student handbooks. Now, I have no argument with establishing appropriate boundaries. The problem comes when those standards carry equal weight with God's standards. When the hippies were no longer a threat, Christians forgot to tear down the fences.

Many of those fences still stand today. How sad to reduce genuine love for Christ to a set of man-made rules and regulations!

The principles of righteousness never change; however, the applications of righteous principles always remain fluid. The well-meaning Pharisees encumbered God's people with the burdens of extrapolated goodness that distracted them from a true love for God.

4. *The better we become, the more we feel God is impressed.* Jesus wasn't impressed with the Pharisees' brand of righteousness. The better they had become on the outside, the worse they had become on the inside. That's why Jesus came down so hard on them. They misrepresented Truth.

JESUS CAME TO PROVE GOD LOVED SINNERS.

The same was true of Simon. His externally spit-polished life blinded him to his true condition.

If we're not careful, we too will equate being good with loving Jesus. When we are honest with ourselves we see an awful lot of Simon in our hearts. Jesus is no more impressed with our whitewashed exteriors than He was with the Pharisees'. You may look like you love Him in your neatly pressed, color-coded Sunday attire, but Jesus knows the real story. Sadly, most of us think that if we pray before every meal (even in restaurants), avoid foul language, teach our kids to tell the truth, cancel our cable, and stop smoking, we've sufficiently demonstrated our love for Christ. As good as keeping the real rules is, "rule-keepers" may miss the point of Luke 7. Jesus affirmed the love

of the one who owed Him the most—the rejected sinner—
not the one who simply kept all the rules.

YOU, TOO, COULD BE A PHARISEE

How do we get into this loveless form of Christianity?
Answer: Self-righteousness blinds. Religious routine kills.
That's why Simon missed seeing the living God in his presence. Why he piously shunned the woman engaged in genuine worship. Why he responded to Jesus from his world of
lists and laws rather than seeing Jesus who was looking for
Simon's love.

What would I do if Christ were to threaten the norms
and traditions of my sense of true religion? Most Pharisees
were both intrigued by and interested in His claims. Simon
no doubt wondered to himself if Jesus could really be the
Messiah. That is the reason for the Pharisees' suspicion of
and uneasiness about Jesus. Their legalistic ways crossed
swords with His brand of gracious, accepting love. Jesus
never condoned sin. But He also never endorsed the Pharisees' burdensome, human-made system of right living.

His teachings reproved them. He challenged the validity
of their traditions. He condemned the pride and hypocrisy
that their goodness had fostered. He confronted their love
for power and control.

Jesus and the Pharisees were miles apart. Jesus came to
prove God loved sinners. The Pharisees believed that sinners
should be condemned. They had no sense of the grace, mercy, and love of God for all mankind. And that failure in their
theology led them to a barren lovelessness that was stained
by an infatuation with themselves and their accomplish-
ments.

A. M. Hunter observes that "the new thing in Christianity is not the doctrine that God saves sinners. No Jew would have denied that. It is the assertion that God loves them and saves them as sinners."[3]

That helps explain why Luke included the story of Simon and the sinning woman. He wanted us to see ourselves somewhere in that scene. It's easy to feel good about ourselves because we have faithfully conformed to what we believe to be are God's ways. It's harder to look at our Christian life from God's perspective.

Granted, you're no Pharisee. I know you desire to serve Christ with an honest and passionate love. More important, God knows that. What I'm advocating is honest reflection about the ways you choose to demonstrate that love for Him and awareness of how quickly we slip from duty to devotion. Are you relying merely on externals to show your love for Christ? Are you ever tempted to think that your goodness is a performance of obligation? Has your goodness become a habit rather than a loving response to grace? Do you believe being good is enough to please God? Do you ever feel a twinge of jealousy toward those more revered than you? Is there hypocrisy or duplicity in your life? Have you ever noticed pride lurking in the shadows of your heart but failed to confront it?

Any "guilty as charged" response to these questions should alert you to the possibility that you've left your first love—you've been co-opted by a system instead of being overwhelmed by the Savior.

One thing is for sure; the "sinning woman" in Luke 7 has a courageous and heartfelt love for Jesus that touched Him deeply. She, not Simon, shows us the way to the joy of loving Christ.

Chapter Two

Bold
Love

THE RADICAL
RESPONSE OF
A GRATEFUL HEART

f rom her youth, Ruth Jordan McBride understood the harsher side of life.

Ruth's father, a Polish immigrant, eked out a living as an itinerant orthodox rabbi in Virginia. Her mother, a shy invalid who spoke broken English, endured frequent beatings from her violent husband. Eventually, Ruth's father gave up on his "calling" and bought a store. Ruth worked long hours and endured stinging verbal attacks and even sexual assaults by her father.

Tragically, Ruth spent most of her adolescent

years looking for love. That search led her down dark and dangerous paths. It ultimately led her straight into the arms of a fella next door—a young black man who had become a regular customer. For the first time in her life she felt cared for. However, this discovery of love proved unsafe. Pregnant and shamed, she felt the scorn of her mother, who quietly sent her away to live in New York with a relative. There the pregnancy would be secretly "dealt with." When she returned home, Ruth made a painful discovery. Life would never again be the same. She went back to New York, where she met Rocky, who also promised love and protection. But he too offered the wrong sort of love—a love that led her into darker places than she had been before. Rocky was a pimp.

Again she fled. Broken, discouraged, and at the end of her rope, the young girl from Virginia had grown strangely old—with a hardness to her that ran deep in her soul. Then she met Dennis McBride—an unusually gentle man who loved her from the start. This time the love was real. She at once felt valued and dignified. She finally belonged.

Still, this love from a man was not enough to deliver her from years of pain and abuse.

Years later, Ruth told her son James the secret—the secret that enabled her to rise like a phoenix out of the ashes of her dad's abuse, a story he writes in the best-selling book *The Color of Water.*

In the book he describes how his mother reflected on the slurs she endured for marrying a black man. She said, "Well, I don't care. Your father changed my life. He taught me about God, who lifted me up and forgave me and made me new. I was lucky to meet him, or I would've been a prostitute or dead. Who knows what would've happened to me? I was reborn in Christ. Had to be, after all I went through."[1]

"Ma was utterly confused about all but one thing: Jesus. . . . Jesus gave Mommy hope. Jesus was Mommy's salvation. Jesus pressed her forward. Each and every Sunday, no matter how tired, depressed or broke, she got up early, dressed in her best, and headed for church."[2]

He continues, "Even as a boy I knew God was all powerful because of Mommy's utter deference to him, and also because she would occasionally do something in church that I never saw her do at home or anywhere else: at some point in the service, usually when the congregation was singing one of her favorite songs like, 'We've Come This Far by Faith' or 'What a Friend We Have in Jesus,' she would bow down her head and weep. It was the only time I saw her cry. 'Why do you cry in church?' I asked her one afternoon after the service. 'Because God makes me happy. . . . I'm crying 'cause I'm happy.'"[3]

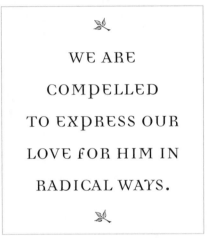

WE ARE COMPELLED TO EXPRESS OUR LOVE FOR HIM IN RADICAL WAYS.

How do the Ruths of this world rise above the debilitating effects of brokenness, abuse, deep emotional burdens, bondage, and temptation, to hold their hands high in victory? Or for that matter, how do any of us escape the stranglehold of a world that, whether in good times or bad, obscures our capacity to live out our love for Jesus?

The answer is clear—and the answer holds our only hope. When those of us who are trapped in the brokenness of life or lost in the comfortable veneer of self-righteous religion come to grips with the true Lover of our souls, we experience radical change. A change that can only be driven by a love for Christ so compelling that it defines all we do—a love defined by the life-changing goodness that only He can bring. When we allow Christ to move us beyond mere mental assent into a vibrant relationship, we are compelled to express our love for Him in radical ways.

That's what happened to Ruth, and that's what happened to the sinning woman in Luke 7. They both met Jesus, and their lives were never the same.

BOLD ADORATION

Ruth McBride's transforming love for Christ is a carbon copy of the experience of the woman that we met in Luke 7. We are introduced to this woman by the Gospel writer who in thirteen verses describes what might be Scripture's most moving and instructive picture of what it means to love Christ. We are never told her name, but we are told that she was a woman "who had lived a sinful life" (Luke 7:37). Luke doesn't say exactly what gave her such a bad reputation, but the word he uses to describe her—*sinner*—is most often used in the Bible to refer to people whose lives were characterized by immorality. She was probably the town prostitute or, at best, a woman known for her loose morals. In ancient Jewish culture, being known as a "sinner" marked people like her as social outcasts. They were the lowest and most despised people in the community.

But her mention in the passage is not the most striking feature of Luke's narrative. We often read in the Gospels of sinners flocking to Jesus. But this woman showed up at Simon the Pharisee's home. Simon had a reputation of his own. He clearly stood out as the best, most religious person in town. A model of piety and godliness. Luke couldn't resist telling the story of how these two starkly different characters wound up in the same room with Jesus.

Luke intends that this sinner-saint encounter marks for us the huge distance between what motivated the sinful woman to act in love and what kept the pious Simon so incapable of truly loving Christ. Luke probes the essence of why it's hard to love Jesus. But this is far more than mere history. This story forces us to consider our own relationship to Him. Of course, we'd want to

> SENSING YOUR NEED TO CHANGE CAN MARK THE BEGINNING OF GENUINE TRANSFORMATION.

see ourselves at the Master's feet worshiping alongside the woman. But in all honesty, we may look more like Simon, enjoying the benefits of His presence, while keeping Him at arm's length!

Now, if you're feeling a bit uncomfortable, don't resist that feeling. It means that we're off to a good start. Sensing your need to change can mark the beginning of genuine transformation.

AMAZING LOVE

As the drama unfolds, we can't help but be amazed at the stunning quality of the woman's love. Courageous, bold, and quick to express itself regardless of risk.

Hearing that Jesus would be dining with Simon the Pharisee, the woman grabbed her most prized possession and made her way to the prestigious gathering. In that culture citizens of a town frequently crowded around the walls or portals of homes where large events took place. Occasions such as Simon's reception would have been a main attraction in the day. Typically held in the large dining rooms or the lush courtyards of the upper class, events like this boasted guest lists that included only the most influential. Just as in our day people stand along sidewalks to get a glimpse of Hollywood's glamorous few, so was the custom then. The doors of Simon's home swung open to anyone who wanted to glimpse into the lives of the rich and famous.

On this high-profile night the topic of discussion likely centered on theology. Jesus' reputation as a powerful teacher of the Law had spread rapidly in the region. What an opportunity for a "town hall meeting" between the young, radical rabbi from Nazareth and the respected Pharisee Simon. For the common citizens of the town, an event like this was an exciting affair in their pre-television, pre-let's-go-to-the-movies world.

WHAT SHE DID NEXT NOT ONLY STOLE THE SHOW BUT DEFIED ALL TRADITION.

So for this woman to be among the onlookers at the dinner struck no one as unusual.

That is, until she stepped through the crowd and inched toward Jesus. You can be sure the room grew silent. The clattering of dinnerware and the chattering of busy servants stopped, side conversations at the table became irrelevant, and the buzzing among the onlookers trailed off into whispers. All eyes were fixed on her. Everyone knew who she was and how she lived. She was "a sinner." As she stepped into the space reserved for the invited guests, a chill must have hit the room. Simon the Pharisee sat stunned. The evening was not going as he had planned.

What she did next not only stole the show but defied all tradition. She continued to make her way to Jesus. Finding Him, she stopped at His feet—where the servant of the house would normally stand—and broke into sobs so deep they released a stream of tears onto the Master's feet. She loosened her hair to wipe His feet, then bowed to kiss them over and over again. As she opened a vile of alabaster and anointed His feet, a heavy, alluring fragrance permeated the room.

Simon was scandalized! Before the meal, he would have performed ritualistic cleansings to purify himself according to the traditions of the code of the Pharisees. For a woman —and particularly a woman of such ill character—to lovingly anoint Jesus in the presence of Simon and his guests violated all sense of religious propriety. It simply wasn't done. Such a bold and beautiful expression of love was incomprehensible coming from someone so obviously unfamiliar with the religious constructs of "goodness."

A rare courage and refreshingly innocent audacity marked her remarkable act of sacrificial love.

THE FRIEND OF SINNERS

Her adoration in plain view of the crowd forced Jesus into a predicament. The crowd's attention had been riveted on the woman; now it suddenly turned to Simon's honored guest. What would He do? After all, His host, proud Simon, held all the power. He set the standards for what was publicly acceptable and what was not. This woman had crossed the boundaries of religious and moral propriety. Jesus risked marginalizing Himself and offending His pompous host if He accepted her. He knew that the religious leaders had already repudiated His teaching. Now they'd have solid proof of His fondness for sinners.

> **BENEATH THE LAYERS OF SIN AND UNSPEAKABLE SHAME, JESUS SENSED HER STUNNING FAITH.**

Let's be honest. It's hard to do what is right when we're under pressure to play to the powerful and privileged among us. We love that kind of approval. Who among us would not have wanted to be accepted by the prestigious group reclining at Simon's table? Jesus could have easily capitalized on the situation. By casting His lot with the power broker Simon, He might have gleaned an endorsement that would have given His ministry a boost.

But, Jesus resisted all that. Without hesitation, He affirmed her outpouring of love and became her Defender and Friend. One thing is clear: The woman's response to Jesus, though radical and culturally abhorrent, touched His heart. Beneath the layers of sin and unspeakable shame, Jesus sensed her stunning faith. Her sacrificial love demonstrated a heart filled with gratitude spilling out onto the One who loved her first. Jesus responded as a merciful Advocate of thankful souls who express genuine love for Him regardless of the cost. He proved that He is indeed a friend of sinners!

What gave rise to the radical and risky expression of love for Jesus that came from this unlikely person? And why was it so easy for such an unrighteous individual to show authentic love for Him and so hard for self-righteous Simon to do so? As we seek answers to these questions, we'll discover what we need in our lives to move from empty religion into an authentic relationship with Christ.

Chapter Three

Life Among the Forgiven Much

❧

LOVING JESUS
THE AUTHENTIC WAY

S imon sat stunned and offended as the woman clung to Jesus' feet. Though he didn't speak, his thoughts betrayed his heart. Luke writes, "When the Pharisee who had invited him saw this, he said to himself, 'If this man were a prophet, he would know who is touching him and what kind of woman she is—that she is a sinner.'"

Luke couldn't resist the irony. Jesus didn't have to hear Simon speak in order to know his heart. He *was* a prophet. Luke simply wrote, "Jesus answered Him, 'Simon, I have something to tell you.'"

Jesus went on to explain the woman's behavior by telling Simon a story of two debtors. One owed a great deal to a moneylender and the other owed considerably less. Neither of them could repay, so the lender graciously forgave their debts. Jesus asked Simon if he knew which debtor would love the moneylender more—the one who was forgiven much, or the one who was forgiven little? Simon responded, "I suppose the one who had the bigger debt canceled." Jesus affirmed Simon's correct response, then went directly to His point.

> ✖
>
> TRUE EXPRESSIONS
> OF LOVE FOR HIM
> FLOW AS A
> SPONTANEOUS AND
> UNSTOPPABLE
> RESPONSE TO
> FORGIVENESS.
>
> ✖

In a withering reproof, He confronted Simon's lack of genuine love. Simon had not extended to Jesus even the most common courtesy granted a guest—foot washing. Nor had he greeted Jesus with the customary kiss. Those acts of courtesy were like my asking you if I might hang up your coat if you were to come to our home in Chicago in the dead of winter. For me not to ask to hang up your coat would imply an unwelcome response to your visit. As we will see, there might have been reasons for Simon to withhold these routine gestures of hospitality, but in this cultural setting his actions would be rude and offensive to any guest, let alone Jesus.

Jesus hadn't missed the snub. In addition to withholding the common courtesies of the day, Simon had denied Jesus the grace of being refreshed with oil. Ordinarily, when guests of honor arrived, they'd be given a special anointing of oil to freshen their faces. Poorer families offered less expensive fragrances for the ritual. Pharisees, on the other hand, anointed their guests with the finest products, demonstrating their prestigious positions in the community. Simon had done none of that.

He hadn't felt it appropriate to honor Jesus with an anointing. Yet this despised woman of the streets washed His feet with her tears and never stopped kissing Him. More remarkably, she brought the most expensive of oils to anoint His travel-weary feet.

Where did her outpouring of love come from? In essence Jesus explains that she is loving Him with such bold affection because she has been forgiven of great sin. Then, for Simon's benefit, He concluded, "But he who has been forgiven little loves little" (Luke 7:47).

> GENUINE LOVE FOR HIM IS ALWAYS A RESPONSE TO HIS EXTREME GRACE EXTENDED TO US.

LOVE AMONG THE MUCH FORGIVEN

Like the debtor in the parable Jesus told, the woman at Christ's feet loved much because she had been forgiven much. Nowhere in Scripture do we find that loving Christ is the *reason* for forgiveness. True expressions of love for Him flow as a spontaneous and unstoppable *response* to forgiveness. Acts of authentic love are a response to Christ's amazing work of grace. It is just that simple. Those who have been forgiven much, love much.

This sinful woman responded to Jesus with a deep and moving love because she belonged to a particular class of people . . . the forgiven much. Those of us who find ourselves in this class live lives fueled by the energy of a deeply indebted desire to express our gratitude through acts of adoring love for Christ. Genuine love for Him is always a response to His extreme grace extended to us.

MARVELOUS GRACE

I wonder what sermon Jesus had preached at this point in His ministry that so deeply impacted the woman's heart. Unfortunately, Luke does not tell us what she heard or saw. But somewhere, at some time, Jesus touched her heart. He met her deepest need, delivering her anguished, exiled soul from fear and despair. Personally, I think Luke hints at when she first encountered Jesus. Earlier in this same chapter, Luke records that about this same time, John the Baptist had sent his disciples to verify Jesus' credentials (Luke 7:18–28). Matthew records those very events in his gospel and clues us into what sermon Jesus preached shortly after John's disciples left Him. And it was a life-changing message indeed!

Stand with this sinful woman in the crowd on that day when the region buzzed with excitement about the arrival of this country preacher from Nazareth. She had heard, perhaps even from a client, about this Jesus who healed the sick and restored sight to the blind. She may have heard, as strange as it would seem to her, that He had proven to be a friend of searching sinners. Coming to join the crowd—for she would have a Zacchaeus type of curiosity (Luke 19:1–4)—she might have strained to see Jesus and hear His voice.

She might have caught a glimpse of His face—a face unlike any she had seen before. Imagine the scene on that green, fruited hillside as it sloped lazily toward the Sea of Galilee. But it is Matthew who records the sermon she most likely heard on that day. Words from heaven like lightning bringing rays of light to her dark and threatened heart.

"Come to me, all you who are weary and burdened, and I will give you rest. Take my yoke upon you and learn from me, for I am gentle and humble in heart, and you will find rest for your souls. For my yoke is easy and my burden is light."

⚜Matthew 11:28–30

Think of what it would mean for *this* woman to hear such a welcoming, forgiving, merciful invitation. It was she who offered rest to men, in encounters that only left her more laden with guilt. No one offered *her* rest. No one cared for her soul. Men used her as an object of desire, only later to ruthlessly discard and condemn her. Any sense of worth and self-esteem were nonexistent in her abused and broken life. She lived under a burden of inextricable guilt, weighed down by the sludge of sin that polluted her soul. No one needed to tell her how lost she was. She lived with that condemning awareness daily.

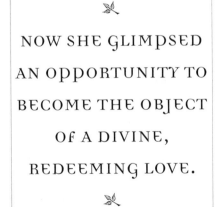

NOW SHE GLIMPSED AN OPPORTUNITY TO BECOME THE OBJECT OF A DIVINE, REDEEMING LOVE.

What she needed was someone to tell her that there was a way out, a way to be forgiven.

And now, for the first time in her life, this desperate woman had come into contact with a man who offered forgiveness and a love she could wholly trust. She must have seen something different in His face. He hadn't offered the looks of sly desire she had seen on the faces of so many other men. She sensed that she could feel safe with Him. Had she finally found someone who cared—someone who wanted, not to use her, but to honor and forgive her?

Later, as the crowd dispersed, she may have lingered to ask about the invitation He gave to anyone who would believe. Could it be that she qualified? Did He really understand who she was? Did it matter—as it had for most of her life? Surprisingly, He was willing to talk with her. His look and His voice raised her hopes that she might find grace in His sight. She heard what for her were almost unbelievable words. Unlike what she had been taught all her life, she heard that God offers mercy and grace and delights in forgiving those who come to Him seeking forgiveness and restoration.

LOVING CHRIST IS A RESPONSE TO HIS ENDURING, UNWARRANTED LOVE FOR US.

She knew in a heartbeat that this was not only what she wanted but also what she needed. For too long she had been the object of men's lusts. Now she glimpsed an opportunity to become the object of a divine, redeeming love. And in a moment of unqualified belief, the sludge that had for so long clogged her soul with guilt and self-incrimination melted away in the cleansing flood of His forgiving grace. The fresh Spirit-breathed sweet air of forgiveness filled and healed her battered soul.

Is it any wonder that when she heard Jesus was dining at the Pharisee's home, she said, "I have to go and see Him once again—to tell Him how much I love Him!" Making her way through the streets that used to be the dark passages of her trade, she set out to express a new kind of love unstained by the past. Arriving at Simon's house, she may have been shocked by the rudeness shown to the Master. And without giving it another thought, she broke from the margins of the room, kneeled before him, and worshiped Him with loving acts that far exceeded even the most careful courtesies Simon could have extended to Jesus.

Why? Because she was among the *forgiven much*. What she did in those moments reflected a moving and instructive response to redeeming love.

For her, as it must be for all of us, adoring expressions of love for Him spring from the life-liberating love He first gives us. He had stunned her heart with His marvelous forgiving grace, and now she responded in gratitude with courageous, reciprocal acts of love.

RESPONSIVE LOVE

Mark it down: Loving Christ is a response—a response to His enduring, unwarranted love for us. His amazing grace motivates us like nothing else to live out our lives in unique and courageous ways that express our deep affection and honor for Him before a watching and often critical world. Why would you or I forgive a parent who had abused us? Why would we give generously to empower the work of Christ? Why do we serve as ushers or sing in the choir? Why would you feed the homeless or take dinner to a sick neighbor? Why would anyone endure a difficult marriage out of conviction that it is the right and honorable thing to do? Why do Sudanese Christians permit themselves to be sold into slavery rather than deny the name of Christ? Why do people leave lucrative and prestigious positions to take lesser tasks in the kingdom work of Christ? Why have martyrs gladly died and others lived in terrible situations with bold, uncompromising spirits? Believe me, such rare selflessness does not arise out of a sense of obligation. Commitment to duty does not provide sufficient resolve. When the chips are down or the stakes are high, mere commitment rarely works.

> ❧
>
> ### SHE NEVER RECOVERED FROM THE IMPACT OF HIS LOVE.
>
> ❧

Since He has lovingly done so much for us, genuine lovers of Christ move quickly from a religion expressed through empty routine to a love marked by unstoppable gratitude. Authentic lovers of Jesus thrive on opportunities to express their love to Him as a living response to His grace.

So if you truly desire to be that kind of Christ-lover you must ask, "Where am I on the continuum between the Pharisee and the immoral woman?" Allow the Holy Spirit to probe your past. When was the last time you were willing to do something radical and dramatic to express your overflowing love for Jesus? Is there a momentum in your soul that pushes toward a deepening, life-altering love for Him, or are you stuck in the cognitive and bound by a codified, passionless arrangement with Him? The answers to these questions determine the authenticity and integrity of your and my claim to love Jesus.

To love Christ—to really love Him—means that, like the sinful woman, we intentionally seek ways to express our love clearly and without intimidation, regardless of the cost. It is gratitude toward a forgiving and grace-extending Savior that drives us to seek out ways to say, "Thank You! This is how much I love You."

FREE AT LAST

Where did Ruth McBride—broken by life and its deep disappointments—get the powerful resolve to live above the brokenness? She found the genuine item in the only One who could fill the gaping hole life had left in her soul. Her life had been dramatically changed by Christ.

Yet, she had one regret. What really bothered Ruth Jordan McBride was her deep guilt for not having gone to be with her mother before she died. While it was true that her family had officially rejected her and refused to tell her where her mother was, Ruth blamed herself for deserting her mom and deeply grieved the lack of closure. Her son recounts Ruth's own words in his book about her life.

> I was depressed for months. I lost weight and couldn't eat and was near suicide. I kept saying, "Why couldn't it have been me that died?". . . Dennis was the one who shook me out of it. He kept saying, "You've got to forgive yourself, Ruth. God forgives you. He'll forgive the most dreaded sin, the most dreaded sin." But I couldn't listen, not for a long while, I couldn't listen. I was so, so sorry. Deep in my heart I was sorry. . . .
> Lord, I was burning with hurt . . . I didn't think she was dying

when I left home, but she knew it. . . . All her life I was the one who translated for her and helped her around, I was her eyes and her ears in America, and when I left . . .well, . . . her husband treated her so bad and divorced her, and her reasons for living just slipped away. It was a bad time.

It took a long time to get over it, but Dennis stuck it out with me, and after a while I began to listen to what he said about God forgiving you and I began to hold on to that, that God will forgive you, will forgive the most dreaded sin.[1]

When Ruth realized that God had lifted the burden of her sin by bearing it Himself on the cross, she turned her eyes and heart toward Him as Savior, Redeemer, Liberator, and Friend. She never recovered from the impact of His love. And she never stopped gratefully expressing it to Him in sacrificial acts of love lavished on an untidy brood of kids whose lives now bless thousands of people.

Ruth lived out her life in the face of great odds as a member of that select group of those who have been *forgiven much*. Her response flowed out of a passionate love for Christ. Her love for Him saw her through the darkest days.

Charles Wesley's timeless hymn "And Can It Be That I Should Gain" catches perhaps better than any other the sentiment of lives lived in the realm of the forgiven much. The sinning woman of Luke 7 and the countless Ruth McBrides of this world might join in grateful chorus in such rare expressions of gratitude and praise. The question is . . . can you?

Long, my imprisoned spirit lay
Fast-bound in sin and nature's night;
Thine eye diffused a quick'ning ray,
I woke, the dungeon flamed with light;
My chains fell off, my heart was free;
I rose, went forth, and followed Thee
Amazing love! How can it be?
That Thou, my God, shouldst die for me!

Chapter Four

Love, the way it was meant to Be

MOVING FROM DUTY TO DEVOTION

My dad loved his garden. My childhood home was on a large tract of land lined by beautiful gardens with dozens of varieties of perennials and my father's favorite rosebushes. He spent much of his leisure time tending and grooming his "little Eden," as he called it. Gardening helped him step out of the stress of his pastoral work if only for a time.

I didn't grow up on a farm. I grew up in North Jersey, where work was having a paper route to make a little extra money and play was with a ball, bat, and glove with buddies at the park. My dad's passion for gardening periodically led to a collision of our interests.

Often—too often for me—my dad would tell me that I needed to spend part of my Saturday with him in the garden. Weeding needed to be done. The flowers had to be deadheaded. There was edging to do and the ever-present drudgery of digging the dandelions out of the lawn. I must say that I usually complied—as though I had a choice—but rarely with a willing spirit. It was particularly painful when my friends rode by on their bikes on the way to the park while I was working in the yard.

> ❧
>
> GOD MEASURES MATURITY BY THE LEVEL OF DEVOTION WE DISPLAY.
>
> ❧

Today I would give anything to have those days back. Now that I am older, I have a far deeper understanding of the significance of my father in my life. I owe so much to him. If I could go back, I would gladly serve with him in the garden, not from the drudgery of duty, but from a heart of devotion. I would even want to get up early and have him find me already at work. From my perspective today, weeding would be a great way to say to my dad, "Thanks for all you have done. I love you!" And Dad would clearly know that I loved him in more ways than words offered in passing and cards sent on Father's Day.

The same is true in our relationship with Christ. As important as the definitions and dogmas are, loving Christ is richer by far than simply coming to grips with the mechanics that attempt to describe our love for Him. If our love is to be true and transforming even in the toughest times, it must be a responsibility that we fulfill as a *response* to His amazing love and marvelous grace poured out in our lives. I'm convinced that's what John had in mind when he wrote, "We love because he first loved us" (1 John 4:19).

DUTY OR DEVOTION?

It seems to me that much of what we do for God arises out of a sense of obligation and duty. Being good is the way we are supposed to be, so we conform. Prone to live out our Christianity at the margins, we sometimes long to be free to play at life as others do. We envy the unrestrained pleasure we see exhibited by those who love themselves, but we dutifully stay in the yard to do the tasks our Father commands. Worse yet, some of us have run from the yard of His love to head for the park where we can play. We fashion our lives after our own dreams and desires—and all the while imagine we are entitled to the benefits of being His child.

Spiritual maturity has to do with *wanting* to do the Father's will for us—not out of duty but out of overriding adoration and devotion. God measures maturity by the level of devotion we display. That devotion becomes evident in our lives when we are gripped with the astounding reality of God's mercy and grace. When we embrace that reality, we gladly serve Him regardless of cost. Authentic Christianity develops out of a gratitude that transforms our lives with unquenchable love. True love—love that is tracking toward the bull's-eye—is a response of devotion to Christ.

THE POWER OF RESPONSIVE LOVE

This kind of loving response to Jesus transforms our attitudes and our behavior. It gives way to spontaneous expressions of devotion. When I was a boy, we sang a song that says this well:

> After all He's done for me,
> How can I do less than give Him my best
> And live for Him completely,
> After all He's done for me.

Unfortunately, we have been schooled to believe that simply "being good" and "doing good" are enough for Christ. We don't often link this behavior with our love for him. Even when we do loving things, we have to admit that we often do them selfishly for recognition, exchange, or honor.

Early in life the importance of "being good" was drilled into my psyche. I would be a wealthy man today if I had gotten a five-dollar bill every time someone said to me, "You're the pastor's son. You have to be good. You are an example to the other children." I didn't want to be an example—I was only five. I wanted to do all the mischievous things my friends were doing. I was good because I *had* to be good.

HE DOESN'T ALLOW US TO REMAIN INFANTS IN OUR RELATIONSHIP WITH HIM.

As adult Christians we feel that same tension. We are good out of duty—it's the right thing to do. After all, we're God's kids and the world is watching. We have been taught that we should "be good" so that we don't disappoint our parents, get caught, and appear hypocritical. The charade continues unchecked. And while those are the downsides of living life on our own terms, Christ-lovers know that these are not the best reasons to be good. Left to that, we will fail to be strong when we think we won't get caught, or we think we can be clever enough to dodge the consequences. That's why it's hard to love Jesus—He doesn't allow us to remain infants in our relationship with Him. He challenges us to go deeper in how we express our genuine love for Him. The right reason to do good springs from the fact that we are in a relationship—a love relationship with Christ. That's the point of Luke 7. The problem is not new. God's people have long suffered from an inadequate sense of religious obligation.

THE PAIN OF A DISCONNECTED LOVE

David, the storied king of Israel, understood that all of life is about a relationship with the Creator. After committing adultery with Bathsheba and arranging the murder of her husband, Uriah, he admitted in brokenness, "Against you, you only, have I sinned" (Psalm 51:4). God had blessed David wonderfully. From his days tending his father's sheep to life as a fugitive on the run from King Saul to the glory years as the anointed one of Israel, David lived as a debtor to God's grace. Yet in David's wrongheaded attempt to secure Bathsheba's love, he violated a covenant with God—a covenant of loyal love.

Not much has changed in three thousand years, has it?

Jennifer Horne loved being at college. She had grown up in a good home and lived within the restraints of a normal Christian family. Being at college was her first time to be on her own, and she was determined to enjoy every minute of it. She was also determined to maintain a solid Christian testimony. That was her duty.

By the second semester she had fallen in love with a great guy—and it didn't take long before the young man started making demands that threatened her moral propriety. All her friends were involved with guys and enjoying their sexual freedom. Still, Jennifer struggled with what her parents would think and with what might happen if she were to become sexually active, or worse, pregnant. Sadly, she worried more about losing her boyfriend than she did about dishonoring God. She had a disconnected love—a religion stuck in duty rather than flourishing in devotion.

Bob Anderson traveled much of the year on business. He loved his wife and family deeply. Yet he found on those lonely nights in the hotel room how easy it was to watch adult movies or to log on to the Internet in search of an illicit thrill. It troubled him when he thought of his wife and position that he held at his church—and rightly so. But it never crossed his mind that his behavior dishonored the Lord and demonstrated how disconnected his faith had become.

Jennifer and Bob both failed to realize that their struggles were more than a test of obedience and being good. These were *love* tests. They measured devotion, not duty. Would they love themselves and their own interests or would they love Christ?

For Bill and Debbie Throckmorton, the toughest challenge of their lives revolved around the thought of forgiving their business partner. To their shock, he had cheated them out of their life savings. Bill and Debbie found it impossible to get past the sense that forgiving him would "let him off the hook." It was more than they wanted to do. In fact, their anger and resentment often felt good—even therapeutic.

Their closest friends affirmed them in their choice not to forgive. To the Throckmortons—good, upstanding church folks—forgiveness was an unreasonable option. They never thought of forgiving their offender as an expression of their devotion to Christ or as a statement of their love for Him.

Barbara Miller understands. As a busy homemaker, she shuttles kids, packs lunches, keeps the house clean, cooks at home to save money, and basically extends her life far past normal levels of energy and strength. Most of her friends work outside their homes, and when they get together in those rare getaway moments for Barbara, they fill the conversation with how much they love their jobs and the diversity and challenge their careers provide. While they never say it, they make Barb feel uncomfortable and alienated. She is gifted and capable too. Even at her worst, if given the chance, she could outdo any of them in the marketplace.

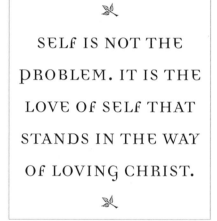

SELF IS NOT THE PROBLEM. IT IS THE LOVE OF SELF THAT STANDS IN THE WAY OF LOVING CHRIST.

Barb and her husband have talked about this on several occasions. He feels that since he makes enough money for them to live on, it is better for the children to have someone at home with them and that someday they will reap the rewards of her sacrifice. For the sake of her kids, she has agreed stay home. She grounds that decision in her belief that God's Word teaches her to complement her husband, graciously supporting him in his role as provider. Though she never feels compelled by her husband to stay home, she feels best doing what she believes God wants her to do.

When long days at home get the best of her, Barbara reminds herself that her response to her husband is really a loving response to the Lord. Her response flows out of devotion, not duty. Her heart is encouraged whenever she thinks of staying at home as an expression of her love for Jesus.

THE SIGNIFICANCE OF SELF

It would be easy to think at this point that loving Christ is about trashing self. After all, isn't self the real enemy? Actually, Jesus taught that self is a valuable player in the enterprise of loving Him (Matthew 22:37). When an expert in the law asked, "Teacher, which is the greatest commandment in the Law?" (v. 36) Jesus replied, "Love the Lord your God with all your heart and with all your soul and with all your mind." He was saying that self is the gift we give to Him. It is the gift He wants. It is the gift that finally proves we love Him.

> IS HE OUR
> COMPELLING
> PRIORITY?

Self becomes a dirty commodity only when we keep it for ourselves and love it more than we love God. Self is not the problem. It is the love of self that stands in the way of loving Christ. In fact, no one can love self and love Christ.

We are not talking about the normal, healthy love of self that motivates us to care and provide for ourselves and to be sure we get enough food and sleep. That's common sense.

God honors that sort of balanced living. What we are talking about is living for self or, worse, yielding to the temptation to serve Christ for self, pretending to serve Him when our real goal is to bring pleasure to self and in the process become disloyal to Him.

Those of us who would rather hold on to self need to know that life spent on self will always become a hollow, destructive existence.

During a two-year imprisonment late in his life, the great British playwright Oscar Wilde wrote a long letter to his homosexual lover—for whom he had left a wife and two children—about the consequences when life is spent on self.

> The gods had given me almost everything. But I let myself be lured into long spells of senseless and sensual ease. . . . I surrounded myself with the smaller natures and the meaner minds. I became the spendthrift of my own genius, and to waste an eternal youth gave me a curious joy. Tired of being on the heights, I deliberately went to the depths in search for new sensation. . . . Desire, at the end, was a malady, or a madness, or both. I grew careless of the lives of others. I took pleasure where it pleased me, and passed on. I forgot that every little action of the common day makes or unmakes character, and that therefore what one has done in the secret chamber one has some day to cry aloud on the housetop. I ceased to be lord over myself. I was no longer the captain of my soul, and I did not know it. I allowed pleasure to dominate me. I ended up in horrible disgrace.[1]

What a tragic end to a life with such brilliant potential!

We should not be surprised that loving Christ is about giving all of self to Him. The greatest complaint I heard from wives when I was a pastor was that they felt they were secondary to their husbands' jobs, sports, TV time, and the evening newspaper. Something about true love makes us want to know where we stand in a relationship. If the one we love loves something else more—oneself or desire or possessions—then we feel that we are not really loved after all.

If we claim to love Christ, then we must demonstrate that love in the stuff of our lives. Do our actions, attitudes, values, and priorities reflect our devotion to Him? Is He our compelling priority, or just one thing among the many things that get a little attention here and a little attention there?

What constitutes true love for Christ? It is an unflinching commitment to yield the totality of myself to His will, wishes, and interests. But most important, it is a commitment driven and defined by my response to the marvelous gift of grace that He has generously showered on my life. By far, the best thing to do with self and with all that self possesses is to give it away as a grateful gift of love. When that happens, the transforming power of love is fully engaged.

> OUR LOVE FOR CHRIST IS REVEALED IN THE TRENCHES, NOT IN THE PEW.

CHOICES OF THE HEART

Allow me to be personal here. Your life is full of choices. As a follower of Christ, your love choices should reflect the most profound relationship you possess—your relationship to Him. Let me probe you with some questions. Do you love that particular temptation or thrill of some private sin more than you love Him? How easily are you able to lay integrity aside in order to achieve financial or professional success? Do you cherish the security and comfort of American culture more than the people Christ may be calling you to serve overseas? Are you more passionate about living your life on your terms than about surrendering your life to His plan?

Only you and God know the answers to those questions. Frankly, being the president of one of the world's most prestigious Christian ministries doesn't let me off the hook. I'm prone to wander down paths of ease and self-preservation too—those insidious passageways that lead only to a house of mirrors. I'm easily tempted to embrace distorted images of myself when I should be focusing on Christ.

Our love for Christ is revealed in the trenches, not in the pew. That truth guarantees that our choices will often be more complex than simple and more demanding than convenient. Loving Christ will often be in contention with the power players of our culture: money, material gain, sensual seductions, position, power, and self-interest. But when we see the choices as a decision between the value of Christ and the value of the competitors, the right decision is clear. The choices we make are the judge of the sincerity of our love.

Christ doesn't just want our heads or the sterile surrender of a will that has been cajoled, frightened, codified, or simply required to obey Him. He isn't impressed with our works if they are done only out of ritual or obligation. To the hardened hearts of the religious folk of His day, He said, "You hypocrites! Isaiah was right when he prophesied about you: 'These people honor me with their lips, but their hearts are far from me'" (Matthew 15:7–8). What a penetrating indictment!

Christ wants our affection. He longs to see the adoration of our hearts. He finds pleasure in followers who willingly join the woman at His feet and express their love to Him in bold acts of loving devotion.

The belief that we must "buck up and love Jesus" and that external patterns of behavior prove our love and loyalty to Christ is a treacherous deception. When we adopt that reasoning, something bad happens on the inside. As we focus on mastering codes of conduct, pride slips in and takes hold. Soon our faith becomes a routine. Ultimately we forget that the real issues of life are defined by what is in our hearts.

> ❧
>
> GOD IS NOT INTERESTED IN OUR LIFESTYLE IF IT DOES NOT BEGIN WITH HEARTSTYLE.
>
> ❧

In my first pastorate, a colleague of mine led a large, prosperous ministry. He was easily—in the best sense of the word—the envy of most pastors in the area. He held high denominational offices and was sought after nationally as a preacher and consultant. External signals of godliness marked his ministry. The kind of haircuts men had, the kind of clothes women wore, one's demeanor and behavior in church, the kind of music played and listened to, the entertainment people enjoyed—those were the hallmarks of his ministry. Once during a statewide meeting he leaned over and said to me, "You know, Joe, your hair is too long to be able to sing in my choir!" Actually, there were probably better reasons that I couldn't sing in his church choir, but I just smiled and said, "Oh really?"

Not long after that, to our shock and disappointment, we learned that this upstanding pastor had abandoned his church and family and had gone to the South to live with a woman he had been counseling. We were astonished at this behavior, given how strict he was about so many things. But had we understood, we might have guessed. He had chosen to measure his commitment to Christ by externals alone. He did his duty. But his devotion was to himself. His love for Christ had become a responsibility expressed in outward conformity.

He has learned from this experience. All of us who know him today rejoice that he and his wife have been reconciled and that, as he himself would tell you, he understands the treachery of empty self-righteousness. He knows that a true love for Christ is not a responsibility but a relationship based on a love for Christ that consumes him.

It shouldn't take such heartbreaking circumstances to move us from duty to devotion. That transformation will come when we wake up to the fact that we too are among the forgiven much.

I am reminded of the wisdom of the writer of the Proverbs who said, "Above all else, guard your heart, for it is the wellspring of life" (Proverbs 4:23). Love as a *responsibility* is about lifestyle. Love as a *response* is about heartstyle. God is not interested in our lifestyle if it does not begin with heartstyle. From God's perspective, lifestyle without heartstyle is no style at all.

Chapter Five

Aspects
of love

LEARNING LOVE
AT THE FEET
OF JESUS

f irst-century Christians were impacted by our heroine, the transformed prostitute who teaches us the patterns of true love. Her adoration of Jesus in the face of hostility and rejection became a powerful example for their own lives. Early Christians were called to exercise their faith and show their love amid life-threatening persecution and rejection from the secular and religious worlds. For them, the tainted woman of Luke 7 who expressed sacrificial love for Jesus in the dining room of Simon the Pharisee became a ready-made hero.

Though two thousand years removed from us, her heroism should still carry clout in our hearts. Yet, she is often a forgotten minor character in the New Testament playlist. At best, her tale receives second billing to the parables of the prodigal son and the Good Samaritan. Yet her story is more our story than theirs. If we had even the smallest glimpse of the depth and breadth of Christ's love for us, we too might be known for such a rare expression of love.

> ❧
>
> IS IT REALLY POSSIBLE TO TOUCH THE DIVINE WITH A LOVE LANGUAGE THAT HE WILL UNDERSTAND?
>
> ❧

Like the woman, we owe much to Christ. He expended His amazing grace to liberate us from hell's grasp. If that weren't enough, He remains the unfailing Provider of a thousand graces every day. He's our Advocate and Defender. He protects us and upholds in the midst of the spiritual oppression we face in our lives. Christ faithfully takes up our cause against offenders. He frees us to love our enemies and live in peace with the world (Romans 12:15–21). Christ fights for us in high places where unseen forces wage war against us. When Satan accuses us before the throne of the Father, Jesus stands to defend us. He alone provides security and confidence in an increasingly hostile environment. He is our helper and friend. And lest we forget, He laid down His life to make it all possible.

All this and more should make us want to break from the crowd of the self-righteous and run to Jesus. To bring Him all we have, to honor Him in loving acts of adoration! What a thrill it would be to sense the hush of the clamor and hear His voice rise to affirm and defend your love for Him! To hear Him silence your enemies . . . to know the peace of resting at His feet! To feel assured that because of Him your life has meaning and purpose.

For all this and more, our hearts reach out to search passionately for ways to demonstrate our love for Him. But how can we love Him? Is it really possible to touch the Divine with a love language that He will understand? What does that kind of love look like?

> GENUINE WORSHIP PROCLAIMS THE WORTH OF THE ONE BEING HONORED.

Let's take a closer look at the love of the broken woman of Luke 7. In that brief encounter at Simon's table an array of remarkable loving qualities poured from her heart. If we wonder how we as mere mortals could ever touch the heart of the Divine, she can show us the way.

LET ME COUNT THE WAYS

Our heroine's bold demonstration of love creates a compelling and challenging pattern for loving Christ. In that pattern we learn five qualities of true love that she demonstrated in her outpouring of grateful love.

A Worshiping Love

When the apostle John wrote in 1 John 3:18, "Let us not love with words or tongue but with actions and in truth," he may have had this woman in mind. She was not content merely to talk about her grateful love for Jesus; she acted it out in concrete ways. Remarkably, Luke gives no indication that she said anything. Yet her sacrificial deed impacts us centuries later. Love that touches Christ proves itself in the reality of our everyday behavior in the workplace, in relationships, and in the handling of our possessions. Authentic love for Christ is an *active* love.

Genuine worship proclaims the worth of the one being honored. It's easy to love Jesus on a formal twice-a-week, Sunday-to-Wednesday schedule. It's hard to love Him daily —in sacrificial, radical expressions of selfless worship. That's the difference.

The mediocrity of our Christianity stands naked and bereft in the light of her bold, adoring love—a love that risked everything to worship Christ.

Making daily sacrifices for the one you love speaks louder than words. In Jesus' day, women cherished perfume. Because the plants and oils from which these fragrances were extracted were rare, even a few drops were costly.

Yet the woman in Luke's story broke an entire jar of prized perfumes and poured it out on Jesus' feet. For her, nothing was too costly for Christ.

Just as Jesus was profoundly moved by this woman's active, loving worship, so He will be moved by the perfume of our lives broken unconditionally at His feet. Unless, of course, we get ensnared in the glory of our own worthiness as exceptional worshipers. That would be the embarrassment of it all—that in seeking to love Him in exceptional ways, we become exceptionally impressed with ourselves. The remedy is to remind ourselves that being counted among the "forgiven much" can never be about us. We aren't even worthy to be forgiven. Perhaps that's why the Bible couches Christ's love for us in terms like *mercy* and *grace*. Even the slightest sense in our hearts that our expressions of love for Christ should be celebrated should warn us of a serious heart problem. We know we are free of self-worship when we love anonymously without regret and regardless of the cost.

The woman in Simon's house sought no honor or recognition. She didn't stage that encounter with Christ to make her way into the Gospels. No, none of that. Her deep gratitude for having been forgiven much drove her to express a deep, rare love for Him. That is why Jesus affirmed her faith.

Her selfless attitude is rare in our self-worshiping, self-absorbed culture. Satisfying flesh-borne desires of wealth and happiness makes it not just *hard* to love Jesus, but *impossible*. We let our motives get skewed by the world's influence. Too often we are motivated to give so that we might be blessed. Too often we choose to serve out of a sense of duty or to keep a clear conscience. That's what the Pharisees did. Instead, genuine love is expressed to Jesus and Jesus alone.

That sort of sacrificial behind-the-scenes love honors Christ and transforms us into genuine worshipers.

A Transforming Love

To the amazement of those in the room, Jesus did not rebuke the woman. But why? Did He perceive that her behavior was not sensually motivated but rather was the only way she knew to express her gratitude? We expect newcomers to the family of faith to know what's "proper." To understand that our love for Christ should be expressed in "appropriate" ways. Jesus appears to be more tolerant than we are. Because of the symbols of her past which she brought to Jesus, her advances could have easily been construed as impure. Still, Jesus affirmed her faith.

She brought to Simon's home her past ways of living and the tools of her trade and laid them at Jesus' feet in an act of purifying surrender. Loosing her hair perhaps signaled a yielding of her past to Him.

That's what I call a transforming love! Christ's love promises to transform you and me too. Bringing it all to His feet becomes a living testimony that we no longer need the shameful stuff of our past to guarantee fulfillment.

Love brings it all: all the foul habits of the past, all the pride, all the self-consumption. Without reservation, regardless of who is watching, in spite of what others may say, Christ-lovers lay everything at His feet. He receives it all and removes it as far as the east is from the west. He is not surprised, repulsed, or shocked by what we bring. He has seen and felt it all before—two thousand years ago when He suffered the blows of our sin. That deserves our highest expressions of adoring love.

I received an e-mail from a radio listener who told me of the years he spent trying to resist the seduction of pornography. Nothing stemmed his appetite. His failure to overcome that temptation left him defeated. After listening to the broadcast, he decided to put a picture of Jesus on his computer screen. Seeing Christ made him aware of the surpassing value of his relationship with Him. In that way he brought his struggle to Christ and willingly laid his desires at His feet. What a marvelous difference that made in his once-defeated life.

This young man had come face-to-face with Christ's transforming love—a first, but essential, step in his journey to freedom.

This would be a good time for you to identify those things that have long kept you in bondage to sin. Transformation only comes when you bring them to Him as gifts of repentance. Do you struggle to control your passions? Do lust and sensuality constantly defeat you? Does greed have its death grip on your heart? Bring it all to His feet. Ask Him to transform each passion into a desire that pleases and glorifies Him. Bring your greed to His feet in a commitment to pursue the gain of His kingdom through generous

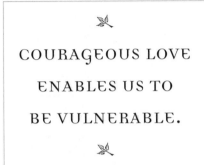

COURAGEOUS LOVE
ENABLES US TO
BE VULNERABLE.

sacrifices of time and resources. Let Him transform your mind to think His thoughts and devise ways to advance His cause. Place at His feet the people you have used and abused for your own purposes, committing yourself instead to serve them for their good and gain.

A Courageous Love

The most obvious aspect of the woman's love is that it was *courageous*. She couldn't have chosen a more hostile forum in which to express her love to Jesus. She lived among the despised and rejected of her day. Luke makes that plain. Still, she chose to enter Simon's house, in the face of ridicule and rejection. But that's where her love thrived. Her love was a courageous love.

Courageous love enables us to be vulnerable. At times when we open ourselves to love we get hurt. It's easy to swear love off and commit never to go there again. We question whether we can become vulnerable again. We wonder if we are willing to open up once more because we love Christ. We ask ourselves if we can trust Him to protect, defend, and reward our love for Him. Do we love Him enough to be willing to be taken advantage of for His sake? After all, we need to remember that He was willing to love us with that kind of courageous, self-denying resolve all the way to the cross.

Mother Theresa loved courageously. Serving for years on the disease-infested streets of Calcutta, she despised the shame and loved unlovable people in Jesus' name. In her later years she became an advocate for the unborn, speaking boldly against the evil of abortion. On one occasion President Clinton invited her to speak at the prayer breakfast held annually in Washington, D.C. The room swelled with dignitaries, including the Clintons and the Gores. Her tiny frame, clothed in a simple cotton sari, seemed out of place in that gathering of influence and prestige. But her words were powerful. Without wavering, she said,

> I feel that the greatest destroyer of peace today is abortion, be-cause it is war against the child, a direct killing of the innocent child, murder by the mother herself. . . . By abortion the mother does not learn to love, but kills even her own child to solve her problems. And by abortion the father is told that he does not have to take any responsibility at all for the child he has brought into the world. That father is likely to put other women into the same trouble. So abortion just leads to more abortion. Any country that accepts abortion is not teaching its people to love, but to use violence to get what they want. This is why the greatest destroyer of love and peace is abortion.

The crowd rose to its feet in thunderous applause while the Clintons and the Gores sat awkwardly staring straight ahead.

They had witnessed courageous love. President Clinton's only reply as the nun from Calcutta exited the platform as quietly as she had arrived was this: "It's hard to argue with a life so well-lived." I would add, "It's hard to dismiss a love so courageously displayed."

It's easy to affirm our commitment to Christ within the safe confines of church or a small-group Bible study. But it's hard to love Him in the hostile arenas of the workplace, or in the face of an offender who needs to be forgiven, or in the presence of a spouse who doesn't share our faith. That takes courageous love.

One woman I know told me that her biggest problem was her Christian friends telling her she was "crazy" to extend grace and mercy to her unfaithful husband. Their advice? "Kick the bum out!" That

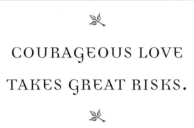

COURAGEOUS LOVE TAKES GREAT RISKS.

would have been the easy thing to do. But Christ-lovers don't just "take in" what everyone else says or thinks. They exercise courageous love and learn to forgive and allow Christ the opportunity to restore trust and wholeness to a broken marriage.

Courageous love takes great risks. When you put yourself at risk to love Him as the woman of Luke 7 did, remember that He *will be* your defender and advocate. Not always in immediate or visible ways. But He will be there, protecting, bestowing grace, and using your love for Him to bring about His ultimate plan. Genuine love for Christ is courageous.

An Advocating Love

It was apparent to this remarkable woman that Jesus was rudely slighted when He arrived at the reception. She saw that He was the only guest who did not have His feet washed, the only guest not to be greeted with a kiss. How could Simon have missed something so important, so basic? Sensing the shame and embarrassment of the insult, she broke from the crowd and headed toward Jesus. Bursting into tears, she washed His feet. She kissed Him and anointed His feet with oil. If no one else would stick up for Christ, she would. Her love for Him refused to let her stand idly by while others discounted His worth. She could not bear such a calculated snub. Her love for Jesus was an advocating love.

Martie and I were enjoying some uniquely Chicago-style pasta dishes in an Italian diner one evening and enjoying a conversation with our server. The server told us she was going on a trip to an Asian country with a friend to discover the teachings of a guru who would bring her, as she put it, "healing and purpose." We listened as she talked about other aspects of her trip. As Martie and I walked home, my heart was burning with conviction. Christ was the answer to her search, and I had not been His advocate among false gods. I was so engaged in the conversation and so taken with the details of her trip that I failed to think of turning her face toward the One I love. It was a low point in my desire to develop a loving relationship with Christ. I had failed as His advocate.

I'm often amazed at how dulled our senses have become to hearing His name cursed. Most shudder to hear the so-called four-letter words, yet they rarely blink an eye at the way Christ's name is used in expletives of anger or disgust.

If anyone spoke against my wife or children—the people I love most—I would not hesitate for a moment to come to their defense. Yet, is that alone the essence of what it means to demonstrate an advocating love for Christ? Most Christians at least wince whenever they hear Christ's name taken in vain. Not unlike the Pharisees, we may go to great lengths to ensure we guard against this violation of God's laws. Yet though we may live our entire lives without speaking His name in vain, we may fail miserably when it comes to being a loving advocate for Him. Loving Christ is about coming to His defense in a world that grants Him no honor. Loving Christ is about loving Him and defending Him in a world that would rather He and all who claim to belong to Him go away. Christ-lovers need not be obnoxious in their defense of Christ but can find appropriate ways to become effective advocates for His name and reputation.

A Personal Love

This woman's love was intensely personal. She had chosen a life of sin, and Jesus offered the solution to her deepest need. He—and no one else—offered acceptance in a community where she had been pushed to the edges without hope of recovery. He became her advocate in a setting where no one else would dare to take her side. She felt no obligation to seek the approval of her critics. She had no need to clear her actions ahead of time. He loved her personally; she would love Him personally in return.

Your love for Christ must be free from restraint—free from the barriers and rules placed on you by others less inclined to love Him. "We love Him because He first loved us." It's that simple. It's that personal.

This was no staged event in Luke 7. This was real. *Refreshingly real.* This is a story about a condemned sinner set free by the love of Christ who showed a grateful love in return—a love that flowed from the depth of her soul. She could not suppress her desire to demonstrate her love. For her it wasn't hard to love Jesus. It was easy because of all He had done for her.

LIFE AT JESUS' FEET

It takes the sinful woman to teach us that life is best lived—most appropriately lived—at Jesus' feet. Her love and repentance drove her to throw herself at His feet in humility. She knew she didn't deserve to be in His presence; she entered as His servant. She demonstrated a true and unassuming love.

In your love for Christ, have you ever assumed that you are doing Him a favor—that He should consider Himself quite blessed to have you loving Him? Have you ever served in a position to be noticed or to leverage power? Must you always be in the spotlight, or would you be content to tell Christ how much you love Him by serving as an usher, a nursery worker, or a volunteer who picks up the sanctuary, sweeps the floors, and cleans the bathrooms after everyone else is gone?

You see, it's hard to love Him when you're more concerned about being noticed and appreciated than you are about responding in humility to His grace.

Can you think of the last time you actively worshiped Christ in an intentional act of love that cost you something? Have you ever brought to Him the symbols of your sinful ways and, in an expression of personal transformation, broken them at His feet? Have you loved Him recently with courage in the face of intimidating circumstances? Is your love strong enough to be willing to become vulnerable for Him? When did you last take up His cause publicly and defend His name? When people see your life do they see your love for Christ?

Overwhelmed? Don't be. We grow in our love for Him. This is not about perfect love. That is what He gave to us. This is about authentically progressing in love for Him. My love for Martie continues to grow deeper even after thirty-four years. The same is true of my love for Christ.

THIS IS NOT ABOUT PERFECT LOVE. THAT IS WHAT HE GAVE TO US. THIS IS ABOUT AUTHENTICALLY PROGRESSING IN LOVE FOR HIM.

I'm not suggesting you master a process. I'm describing a passion to be expressed. Our heroine didn't check the list in her pocket to make sure she covered all the points in her adoring gestures of love. She simply seized the opportunity, and He loved and defended her for it.

Her love challenges me. It sets a high mark that provides a target to shoot for. But I must admit that as much as her love challenges me, Simon's attitude convicts me. A look at Simon's attitudes and the reason for them helps to explain why it's so hard to love Him when we've never really accepted His love to begin with.

simonized
saints

SYMPTOMS OF
A LOVELESS LIFE

Seeing ourselves as we really are is difficult. We rationalize and excuse our weaknesses and sins. We quickly forget the conviction of the Word. We resist the accurate criticisms of our spouse or friends. We tend to wrap our lives in a shroud of self-deception that keeps us feeling good about ourselves. In effect, we become simonized saints.

Simon is the Pharisee in Luke 7. Unfortunately, we never see a successful Simon. He didn't get it. In fact, he would have been shocked to think that his life did not please God. His preoccupation with his own goodness and his lack of love for Christ may give us a clue about ourselves—that is, if we are willing to see ourselves in the mirror of his well-intentioned but deeply flawed attitudes.

We have all seen people on beaches and in other public places strangely dressed. You wonder if they've ever looked in a mirror. After sitting in church behind a lady in an outrageous hat, Robert Burns, the Scottish poet, couldn't resist writing,

> *Would to God the gift to give us*
> *To see ourselves as others see us.*

My wife, Martie, had been after me for months about my putting on weight. Like Simon, I didn't get it. I felt fine, ate well, and slept well, and my friends still liked me—so what was the big deal? One day after showering I caught a glance of my frame in the bathroom mirror. That reality check made me admit that Martie had a point. I needed to change my life habits.

The image of Simon in Luke 7 is like that mirror. It lets us see ourselves as God sees us. We may not be exact replicas of Simon, but his self-absorbed response to Christ might cause us to see our own loveless rituals and religious habits.

Have you ever wondered why Simon invited Jesus to dinner in the first place? As an astute Pharisee, Simon knew how popular Jesus had become. He viewed the young rabbi's teaching as radical and dangerous. The large following Jesus generated threatened the power base Simon had worked hard to maintain. Jesus' fresh teaching on love and kindness made the codes and traditions Simon represented sound stuffy and bureaucratic.

Simon understood what it would mean for Jesus to visit

his town. The ramifications could be huge. An encounter with this traveling teacher from Nazareth was sure to impact him personally. Perhaps that's what he feared most.

When we begin opening our lives fully to Him, He desires a level of access that threatens our control. We don't like Him to get too close. Simon didn't either. If the townspeople were to adopt the teachings of Jesus and turn their hearts to follow Him, Simon and his religious system would lose out big time. Sadly, his entrenched perspective blinded him to what he stood to gain. He failed to understand that by releasing all he once thought profitable he would open the door to the surpassing greatness of knowing Christ (Philippians 3:7–8).

OUR TEMPTATIONS COME IN MORE SUBTLE FORMS.

Someone has said, "In times of battle, stay close to your friends . . . but stay even closer to your enemies." Perhaps that entered Simon's mind when he decided to invite Jesus to dinner.

AN UNUSUAL DINNER GUEST

So don't assume that this invitation arose from Simon's desire to honor Jesus. No, this was more likely a purely political move—an attempt to align himself with what was fast becoming a grassroots phenomenon.

Still, I'm tempted though to think that something about Jesus intrigued Simon. Jesus demonstrated unusual insight into the Scriptures. It's actually possible that Simon, like

Nicodemus, was a genuine seeker. If the evening went as planned, Simon could see for himself what Jesus had to offer.

But an invitation to Jesus was not without risk.

Even so, Simon made a move toward Jesus. In doing this, he stood on the brink. He was asking the potential Redeemer of his soul to be a guest at his table. This was the most important dinner party he would ever throw.

THE COMfORTABLE DISTANCE

Luke skillfully demonstrates Simon's indifference to Christ. Simon intended to keep Jesus at a comfortable distance. Jesus' presence would not be allowed to threaten his position, power, or standing among friends and colleagues. Simon's was an attempt to appear associated with Jesus without losing control.

Many Christians adopt the same strategy. We don't like to have our space invaded either. We enjoy a level of control over the decisions we make about spending money, raising our kids, and making plans for the future. It's hard to let Jesus have full access. He's more useful to us as a fair-weather friend.

That's the danger. Rarely are Christians tempted to openly deny Jesus. Our temptations come in more subtle forms.

My role as a Bible college president means I travel frequently. Most often I fly, and when I do, I enjoy reading my Bible during the flight. I always wonder what the passenger next to me thinks about that. Any discomfort I feel betrays my own temptation to hide my identification with Christ. In the workplace you might face that same struggle. Let's be honest. Some relationships would evaporate before our eyes if we let our love for Christ manage our values and actions. Our dreams and plans could be threatened. The drive to achieve and accumulate would soon fade in the fresh light of an open commitment to Christ. Rather than risk losing all that, we choose to keep Him at arm's length. Not in one grand choice, but in small, seemingly insignificant choices we make every day. But those minor denials add up to major ones. Before long, our hearts grow dull to the passion of an unbending commitment to Christ. When the real test comes, our weakened defenses give way and we succumb.

Archbishop Thomas Cranmer lived during the tumultuous days of the Reformation. Many Christians in England gave their lives for the name of Christ. Just after the coronation of the Roman Catholic queen, Mary Tudor—or "Bloody Mary," as she was called—Cranmer was arrested and spent three years in prison. The queen's emissaries urged him to recant his faith and pledge allegiance to the pope and Rome's doctrine. He was an old man then, and the thought of being burned at the stake was more than he could bear. He signed papers of recantation in order to gain freedom. Later, at the event celebrating his release, he prayed openly:

O Son of God, Redeemer of the World . . .
Have mercy upon me most . . . miserable sinner,
I, who have offended more grievously than any can express.
Whither should I flee for succour? . . . I find no refuge . . .
O God the Son . . .
Although my sins be great, yet Thy Mercy is greater.
I crave nothing, O Lord, for mine own merits,
But for Thy name's sake, that it may be glorified thereby,
And for Thy Dear Son Jesus Christ's sake.

Then, to the shock of all who had packed the church that day, Cranmer said,

> My hand has offended in writing contrary to my heart. There-fore, my hand shall be the first punished, for if I may come to the fire it shall be burned first.[1]

> DO YOU RELATE TO CHRIST ON THE BASIS OF WHAT HE CAN DO FOR YOU?

After canceling the earlier recantation of his faith, he was led to the fire, where he died for what he could not deny. For him, even the flames of a cruel and painful death were not enough to distance his grateful heart from the One who had loved him first.

We can understand why Archbishop Cranmer would struggle at the point of life and death. It is much harder to understand why we would struggle with far less intimidation.

Think of the hypocrisy of claiming to love Christ while maintaining a convenient distance from Him. True love is complete, not merely convenient love.

WHERE'S THE PARTY?

Martie and I are often in social settings where people approach us and engage me in conversation without even acknowledging her. They rarely look her way, say hello, or extend the courtesy of a smile. They see she's there but don't recognize that she's important. The truth is that if these people knew her and how pivotal her influence is on my life, they would find conversation with her far more worth their while than conversation with me.

This is something like what happens with Christ. We notice that He's present but we don't recognize His value.

Simon wrongly assumed that the party was at *his* table. But the real party in his home took place at the feet of Jesus. Simon's self-righteousness blinded him to that fact. He thought more about how this visit from Jesus would benefit him. Having the clout to get Jesus to the table was a feather in Simon's power-cap: He thought that Jesus was coming to his table on his terms and for his glory.

Do you relate to Christ on the basis of what He can do for you? Is life your party to which Christ has come? Is your relationship with Christ about bringing you peace, comfort, fulfillment, and blessing? If so, you don't get it either. The psalmist of old had a clearer perspective when he exclaimed,

> *Shout for joy to the LORD, all the earth.*
> *Worship the LORD with gladness;*
> *come before him with joyful songs.*
> *Know that the LORD is God.*
> *It is he who made us, and we are his;*
> *we are his people, the sheep of his pasture.*
>
> *Enter his gates with thanksgiving*
> *and his courts with praise;*
> *give thanks to him and praise his name.*
> *For the LORD is good and his love endures forever;*
> *his faithfulness continues through all generations.*
>
> ✄ Psalm 100

Now that's my kind of party—where we're the guests and God is the center of attention of the entire universe!

> LOVING CHRIST IS ABOUT LIVING LIFE AT HIS FEET, NOT ABOUT HAVING HIM SIT WITH US AT OUR TABLE. UNTIL WE ABSORB THAT REALITY, WE WILL BE TEMPTED TO *USE* HIM, NOT *LOVE* HIM.

Simon was the only one at the center of his universe. This repulsive woman from the streets and her shocking behavior stole his show. She knew the real life of the party and chose to fall at His feet in loving worship. Had Simon done the same, his eyes would have been opened to the truth. But this was "his party," and Jesus had not followed the script. That's the point of Luke 7.

Christ *is* the party! We should trust and endorse what He does in our lives by demonstrating unflinching allegiance to Him. We should get past thinking that life is one big party for us. Yet it usually takes adversity or some heartbreaking event to bring us to reality.

One of the most difficult things I ever did as a pastor was to tell a church member that her husband, son, and father-in-law had drowned in a boating accident. The loss to her and her entire family was unimaginable.

As the days following the accident unfolded, I watched with admiration as these dear people faced this great and unexplainable loss with unusual faith. Broken, confused, and devastated, they still kept their eyes fixed on Christ. There's only one explanation for that sort of resolve. They embraced what Simon chose to ignore. They didn't live expecting Christ to offer life on their terms. Instead, they chose to trust Christ as the loyal lover of their souls.

One summer Sunday I slipped into the back row of a small country church. After a season of praise and worship, the pastor asked a woman to come forward to offer what he called "prayers for the church." She had come prepared. She prayed tenderly: "And, Lord, we pray this morning for Susan and Peter . . ." At this point her voice broke, and after failing to get the next couple of words out, she stopped. Following a few awkward moments, she regained her composure and continued. "Lord, we don't know why You have seen fit to take three children from our church family in the last year."

I sat stunned by what I'd heard—three deaths of children in that small church? I swallowed hard as she continued with a prayer I will never forget: "But, Lord, we know that it is not ours to ask why, but to trust You. So, Lord, teach us to trust."

That kind of complete trust in Christ amidst devastating loss is unexplainable apart from an unshakable love for Christ.

Loving Christ is about living life at His feet, not about having Him sit with us at our table. Until we absorb that reality, we will be tempted to *use* Him, not *love* Him.

SIMONIZED SAINTS OR SURRENDERED SERVANTS?

Though disastrous for Simon, the sinning woman's actions provided the moment he had hoped for. Simon now had Exhibit A to prove that Christ was a fraud. Simon said to himself, "If this man were a prophet, he would know who is touching him and what kind of woman she is—that she is a sinner" (Luke 7:39).

As quickly as the accusation formed in Simon's mind, Jesus burst the bubble. He turned to His startled host and said, "Simon, I have something to tell you."

"Two men owed money to a certain moneylender. One owed him five hundred denari, and the other fifty. Neither of them had the money to pay him back, so he canceled the debts of both. Now which of them will love him more?"

To which Simon replied, "I suppose the one who had the bigger debt canceled." And Jesus said, "You have judged correctly." Jesus then turned to the woman, but continued to speak to Simon.

"Do you see this woman? I came into your house. You did not give me any water for my feet, but she wet my feet with her tears and wiped them with her hair. You did not give me a kiss, but this woman, from the time I entered, has not stopped kissing my feet. You did not put oil on my head, but she has poured perfume on my feet."

⊱Luke 7:40–46

You might be tempted to think that Jesus was really saying, "Look, Simon, you're a pretty good guy. You don't live on the dark side of life. You are not in the grip of addictions. In fact, Simon, you have a reputation for keeping all the laws and codes to the letter. You and I stand as colleagues in this enterprise of righteousness. I'm proud of you, Simon, and since there is not much in your life to forgive, I don't expect you to love me all that much."

Jesus had Simon's number. He knew the evil of his system of religion. He confronted it systematically in His ministry. The Pharisees took pride in their righteousness and because of that were deeply offensive to God. The trappings of their complicated religiosity veiled their spiritual emptiness. But Jesus saw through the façade. He knew that an inner lust for power would soon energize them into conspiring with Rome to have Him violently eliminated.

Jesus condemned their well-practiced lives and showed little tolerance for their public strutting of their holiness. He condemned the hypocrisy of their well-practiced lives. "Woe to you, teachers of the law and Pharisees, you hypocrites! You are like whitewashed tombs, which look beautiful on the outside but on the inside are full of . . . everything unclean" (Matthew 23:27).

> A TRANSFORMED LIFE CAN ONLY COME WHEN WE GRASP THE DEPTH OF OUR SIN AND THE DEPTH OF GOD'S GRACE.

Those of us who tend to be simonized saints are not much different. Jesus sees through the veneer of our passionless faith and puts His finger on our hearts. He tells us what He was telling Simon: "You don't think you need to be forgiven much. And because you don't feel you need to be forgiven much, you do not love me much."

If we're not careful, our masks of religious conformity will keep us from seeing our true selves. We will get trapped into thinking that as long as everyone else is convinced we're good Christians, the real story doesn't matter.

I accepted Christ as Savior when I was six. I grew up in a Christian home and have served Him in ministry most of my life. It is hard to see myself among the "forgiven much" —and that makes me too much like Simon.

The loving gratitude that results in a transformed life can only come when we grasp the depth of our sin and the depth of God's grace. Let's face it: Getting a love-stirring grip on God's grace comes hard when we live lives of ease and comfort. That combination of comfortable living and superficial faith can be lethal. When we succumb to it we become little more than religious robots, mechanically bound to programmed actions and responses. Like Simon, we grow indifferent to His presence. God wants a grace-born affection that drives us to spontaneous, sometimes risky, and even radical expressions of love.

Without a deepening awareness of why grace is essential, we are lulled into developing an exaggerated perspective of our own worthiness. After all, none of us is as bad as the next guy and certainly not as bad as the condemned criminal. We who have lived in the church culture for so long have put our lives into fairly decent shape. We keep the rules, say the right things, serve, sit, soak, and feel quite satisfied. But that misses the point. Keeping the rules and living moral lives falls short of what Christ wants for us.

Jesus might say to you and to me what He said to Simon: "You don't love Me much because you don't believe you have been forgiven much." That's a stinging reproof! One that should cause us to seek a renewed and realistic view of how sinful we really are and to never forget that we too, all of us, are among the forgiven much.

Chapter Seven

Barriers to Love

OVERCOMING SELF THROUGH SACRIFICE

In the world of violins, a Stradivarius has no peers.

The great violin maker, Stradivarius, had a touch like no other in his trade. Three hundred years after his death, his violins remain exceptional in tone, quality, and playability. Artists around the world hold him and his remarkable craftsmanship in highest esteem. The few violins bearing his name can be worth hundreds of thousands of dollars. Many of them are kept in well-secured display cases in museums. On rare occasions they are issued to a select few virtuosos who demonstrate their worth in spellbinding performances.

If a Stradivarius violin could talk, it would no doubt tell of the joy and beauty of the life it owed to the master-craftsman. But it would also tell of its obscure beginnings in the sludge of a polluted harbor in Cremona, Italy, where Antonius Stradivarius lived.

THE PIT FROM WHICH WE HAVE BEEN DUG

Loving Christ is most often sabotaged by our not knowing or, worse yet, forgetting where we would be today had our Master not transformed us.

When we trivialize our true condition and downplay our need of God's grace, expressing a love born of gratitude like the woman in Luke 7 is an impossible task. We end up like Simon—convinced we're the genuine item but far from what God desires.

> LOVING HIM SACRIFICIALLY MEANS UNDERSTANDING HOW DESPERATE WE WERE BEFORE SALVATION.

Life in Chicago affords real-life examples of Christ's power to transform a life. Many of my friends are street warriors who take the liberating message of Christ to the city's most despairing souls. On occasion I hear their testimonies. They tell heart-warming tales of Christ airlifting them from the desperate places of their lives and placing them on solid ground.

Arloa Sutter founded Breakthrough Ministries, which brings the love of Jesus to the homeless of Chicago. Many have been destroyed by poor choices or victimized since birth. They are painful pictures of sin's life-destroying power. At a banquet celebrating Arloa's ministry, a man gave his testimony. He told of the deep change Christ brought to his life. Arloa glowed with joy. She related that this man had lived for years as a vagrant. But since becoming a Christian he had found full-time work and lives in his own apartment. Daily he witnesses to others about the life-changing power of Christ's love.

Stories of radical redemption leave me feeling cheated. People with those sorts of dramatic conversions weep with joy at what Christ has done. Their lives are driven by heartfelt love, and they live each day grateful for His love. They seem to have the edge on those of us who have experienced less dramatic rescues. To think that we haven't been saved from much leaves us feeling we really haven't been forgiven much.

Yet we *have* been forgiven much. Loving Him sacrificially means understanding how desperate we were before salvation and experiencing God's inexhaustible mercy and grace.

Sadly, though, our splintered lives keep us from such honest reflection. We focus more on externals than on the heart. We spend money to enhance our image. We work hard to preserve the levels of comfort and luxury to which we've grown accustomed. It requires a revolutionary reality check to see ourselves as bankrupt sinners before a pure and just God. Yet we'll never grow in our love for Christ until we make that fundamental change in our thinking.

I was in our employee coffee shop when a colleague casually greeted me with the familiar, "How are you today?"

To which I replied, "Better than I deserve."

"Oh no, you deserve a lot" was his gracious reply. But to

be honest, I had to respond, "Actually, I deserve hell, so everything today beyond that is a bonus."

He was taken back by that—but he shouldn't have been.

You may be thinking, *I don't like to trash myself and go through life thinking that I am nothing.* That's just the point. Sin did that for you! You've been trashed by sin, debilitated by its bondage since birth. That's why Jesus came. Paul, the great first-century apostle, wrote, "For he has rescued us from the dominion of darkness and brought us into the kingdom of the Son he loves, in whom we have redemption, the forgiveness of sins" (Colossians 1:13–14). Like the priceless violins, we were deadwood in the swampland of sin until the Master transformed us into instruments of His grace!

What we need is some fresh perspective. I'm convinced three obstacles keep us looking more like Simon than the grateful woman at Jesus' feet.

Parentage

As a boy Simon no doubt went regularly to study at the feet of local rabbis and Pharisees. His life was formed and framed by the Hebrew Scriptures. He learned early on the importance of adhering strictly to the codes and regulations of the Pharisees. He grew up believing his pedigree and training were sufficient to keep him in good favor with God.

Christians can fall into the same trap.

As I have mentioned, I accepted Christ at the age of six. So the bad things I was redeemed from consisted of biting my sister and not picking up my room. Being a third-generation follower, I could do the church thing blindfolded with my hands tied behind my back. Jesus was a side matter. As long as I stayed the course my parents set for me, I'd be fine.

To grow up in a Christian home was a blessing. But I have also faced the temptation to take my salvation for granted, to forget how far Christ has had to bring me.

My gratitude for Jesus has grown deeper as I've gotten older. I tremble to think of what might have been if I had not been touched by His grace. I wonder what my self-centeredness might have done to treasured relationships with Martie, my children, and my friends. Thankfully, along the way the Spirit has continually nudged me toward maintaining a genuine sense of humility and gratitude. Responding properly to those nudges remains a daily challenge. Likely, you've experienced them too.

I find thinking about what might have been is a valuable spiritual discipline. The clearer our understanding of our own desperate need for Christ, the deeper our expressions of love will become.

My street friends and others who have been radically transformed have nothing on me after all. I, too, am a debtor. In fact, the amazing grace bestowed on me in my being born into a godly home, getting an early start, and being shielded from the horror and pain others have experienced gives me great reason to love Him deeply.

Position

Another obstacle is *position*. As a religious leader Simon enjoyed being looked up to as a model of righteousness. His own depravity—a deep sense of his spiritual bankruptcy—never crossed his mind. Accolades and applause from those beneath him only reinforced his delusion. High religious position is a tricky business.

Some people feel I must be a fairly good person to be

president of the Moody Bible Institute. But it's not me; it's the position they see. Positions of influence, especially spiritual influence, too often mesmerize people. Pastors, Bible teachers, church elders, philanthropists, and other high-profile spiritual leaders face that all the time. If we are not careful, we begin to put stock in our position too—that somehow our elevated status reflects a better standing before God.

Nothing could be further from the truth!

That had to be part of Simon's struggle. How could he admit his need for the Savior and join the woman at Jesus' feet? To do that would suggest he needed to submit to Jesus. His system demanded that others submit to him. People who did what he did were not the ones who needed saving. In fact, the Pharisees held the prerogative to sit in judgment. No wonder Jesus called them blind guides! Simon's position as the lead religious guy in town put him at a grave disadvantage when it came to understanding who Christ was and why he needed Him so desperately.

>
>
> WE SLIP INTO
> A SYSTEM OF
> RELIGIOUS SCORE
> KEEPING.
>
>

How different from what the Bible teaches. Scripture teaches that when some of God's highly positioned people came into His presence, they were struck with the depth of their sinfulness. Isaiah froze in his tracks as a dead man and immediately felt the pain of his sin (Isaiah 6:1–6). The apostle John fell before Christ in terror and fear (Revelation 1:17). Peter, shamed by his own sinfulness, fell prostrate at Christ's feet (Luke 5:8).

In contrast, Simon brooded in his seat of honor at the banquet while the Creator of the universe dined at his table! His position blocked his view.

The Point System

A misconception among Christians is that the sin problem is about how many sins we commit. We slip into a system of religious score keeping. That may have been Simon's problem too. In his mind, he didn't have to be forgiven much. His sin count would have been admirably low, on some days even zero.

Most of us do the same. We measure our sinfulness by counting our sins or by comparing our sins with sins of others. There's always someone who sins more than we do. And that makes us feel better to have the lower score.

But it's not the *number* of sins we commit that offends God. It is the fact that *we are sinners* who need to be reconciled to God (Ephesians 2:1–10).

I am reminded of the man who upon arriving in heaven noticed that all the clocks had names under them. He asked Peter, who seemed to be the Q&A resource in heaven,

> IT'S EASY TO WAG MY RIGHTEOUS FINGERS AT THOSE WHO CONSORT WITH IMMORALITY. IT'S HARDER TO COUNT MYSELF AMONG THOSE IN NEED OF CHRIST'S GRACE.

"What's with all the clocks?" Peter answered that they were

not clocks but "sin meters." He noticed that Billy Graham's hardly ever moved. The pope's seemed to be motionless as well. The meters of other well-known people moved very little. The man asked Peter, "Does Stowell have a clock?" To which Peter replied, "It's in the office. We use it as a fan." I love that joke! Mainly because it's more truth than fiction.

We are sinners and within us lurks the potential for every heinous sin in the book. We take pride in our outrage at the lawlessness of the godless. People like that are everywhere in the entertainment industry, the political arena, and big business. But they're also in the church! It's easy to wag my righteous fingers at those who consort with immorality. It's harder to count myself among those in need of Christ's grace.

You and I could be the rapists, the child abusers, and the serial killers that shock the world with their disregard for morality and justice. Yet, it is God who has given us godly homes, churches, and fellow believers to hold us accountable. If it weren't for the indwelling Spirit and the Word of God to guide, reprove, teach, and correct us, we could rank among the worst of them. We carry all the seeds of sin. The difference is that we belong to those "forgiven much."

If life to us is about counting our sins and comparing ourselves to others, we will find it hard to love Jesus sacrificially. But if we realize that it is our own sinful ways that nailed Him to the cross, we will never recover from His mercy.

I like the way the hymn writer puts it:

> *My sin—O the bliss of this glorious thought—*
> *My sin, not in part, but the whole,*

Is nailed to the cross, and I bear it no more:
Praise the Lord, praise the Lord, O my soul!

Getting beyond our parentage and position and the point system of counting our sins will come through God's grace and through what we do in the daily routines and encounters of life. At the crossroads of a compelling temptation, do we stop to ask whether we love Him more than the temptation? When we hear His call to step out in radical, risky acts of obedience, do we think of His sacrifice for us? Does the power of that thought propel us past our fears to respond in radical obedience?

There is a road back from that faulty living. We can rekindle our love for Him. We can reclaim the affection that will deliver us from the stale and sterile experiences of a loveless faith!

That will require us to renew our minds. To deal honestly with distortions that deceive us into thinking too well of ourselves. To no longer rely on parentage, position, and a point system to give us right standing before God.

Like Simon, when we think too much of ourselves we end up with an oversized me. The remedy? A healthy *fear of God.*

> THE DRAMATIC CONTRAST BETWEEN OUR FALLEN FRAILTY AND GOD'S PERFECT PURITY PUTS HIS TENDER MERCY IN BOLD RELIEF.

THE FEAR OF THE LORD
IS THE BEGINNING . . .

Psalm 111:10 says, "The fear of the LORD is the beginning of wisdom." This fear the psalm speaks of is more than simply fright. It is reverential awe. The Bible does not call us to love God because we are afraid of Him—but to be in awe of Him and obey Him because we love Him.

Count on it. We won't be struck with awe and adoration until we know the magnificence and wonder of His being. And we will never comprehend our deep sinfulness until we have seen the blazing purity of His holiness. The dramatic contrast between our fallen frailty and God's perfect purity puts His tender mercy in bold relief.

> UNTIL WE SEE GOD IN HIS TERRIFYING SIZE AND LIMITLESS SCOPE, WE WILL NEVER SEE OURSELVES AS WE REALLY ARE.

In Deuteronomy 6:1–5 God reveals the foundational way for relating to Him. Three issues are put forward: fear the Lord, affirm that He is the only God, and love the Lord your God with all your heart, soul, and strength. If we are to turn our hearts toward loving Christ, we must cultivate a genuine reverence for God.

It's hard to love Jesus in this way in a world that encourages a small view of God.

Gone are the awe-inspiring cathedrals and the echoing sounds of great organs that draw our hearts to a transcendent God. A God who exists infinitely bigger than ourselves. Today many Christians worship in comfortable, living-room-type churches that when taken to the extreme seem more human-centered than God-centered. We hear soothing messages of a God who lovingly accepts us and tolerates our whims and weaknesses. One pastor who has a global television ministry was even quoted as saying,

> I don't think that anything has been done in the name of Christ and under the banner of Christianity that has proven more destructive to human personality, and hence counter-productive to the evangelistic enterprise, than the un-Christian, uncouth strategy of attempting to make people aware of their lost and sinful condition.[1]

We are encouraged to see God as a companion who will fit into our "buddy system." Sort of a divine ATM designed to respond to any number of impulses. When He doesn't perform, we get irritated and threaten to discard Him.

Barbara Ehrenreich observed in *Time* magazine that "our desire to make the awesome adorable is spoiling the mysteries of life." She pointed out how NASA dumbed down their communications by giving goofy names to rocks collected on the probe to Mars. They called them names like Yogi, Scooby-Doo, and Barnacle Bill—as though "someone high up in NASA must have issued a firm directive: 'Keep it cuddly, guys . . .'"[2]

Then she went after the church:

> Watch one of those schlockier televangelists, and you'll be introduced to an affable deity eager to be enlisted as your

personal genie. Yes, the Great Spinner of Galaxies, Digger of Black Holes is available, for a suitable "love offering," to relieve the itch of hemorrhoids and help you prevail in office intrigues! . . .

At least the ancient Hebrews had the good sense to make Yahweh unnamable and unseeable except in the flames of the burning bush—a permanent mystery.[3]

Tough words coming from an outside observer! The truth hurts.

Until we see God in His terrifying size and limitless scope, we will never see ourselves as we really are. Nor will we fully appreciate the fact that He chose to love you and me. We must ask the question the little girl asked her dad as they watched planes fly overhead and get smaller and smaller as they climbed into the sky. When she finally took a plane trip with her family, she grew increasingly pensive and asked her father, "Are we small yet?"

Not a bad question for Christians to ask regularly. Are we small yet?

When we see God as He is we realize we are small.

Jerome Miller wrote:

Standing before what I experience as ultimately Sacred, I myself am compelled to acknowledge that in and of myself I am precisely nothing. Before the Sacred, I feel, in and of myself, utterly insignificant, utterly without substance. I cannot take myself seriously.

He notes that the only response we can have in the face of God is "terror, which is itself fear rendered acute and panicky by an imminent danger, has, of course, always been recognized as an appropriate response to the Sacred."[4]

When was the last time you thought of God in those terms?

We have long forgotten that even our good works in the light of His holy presence are like trash (Isaiah 64:6). Yet we insist on parading them as a badges of honor. You and I could point out the times we have said no to temptation and yes to the really hard things He has asked us to do. But He is not impressed. Under the shining spotlight of His holiness our desperate condition comes into view.

Any thoughts that upon seeing Him we might hug Him, high-five Him, or bombard Him with a list of nagging theological questions are absurd. Instead, we will be compelled to fall on our face before Him and beg for His mercy.

When we understand that, something wonderful happens.

Instead of annihilating us, He reaches to us in love and touches us with cleansing grace. He adopts us as His children, grants us an inheritance, and offers us unlimited access to His presence. He fills our trembling hearts with hope, confidence, and courage and promises to deliver us to an eternity in His presence.

Christ-lovers never lose sight of the wonder of it all. They never fully recover from experiencing His presence. Nor do Christ-lovers forget the touch of His healing grace and

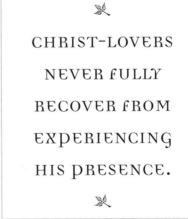

CHRIST-LOVERS
NEVER FULLY
RECOVER FROM
EXPERIENCING
HIS PRESENCE.

mercy. Once they see Him and experience Him, their lives are never the same. Their hearts are filled with unquenchable affection and adoration. That's what happened to the woman in Luke's story. And it can happen to you too.

FROM SELF TO SACRIFICE

For centuries the Stradivarius violin remained a mystery. Why would just one violin maker do what no one else could do? There is a theory that Stradivarius took most of the wood used to carve his instruments from the polluted harbor near his home. That wood had soaked there for years—choice wood used for centuries to fashion oars, boats, and other items necessary for sea trade. Broken and abandoned in the harbor, the wood fell victim to the decay-infested microbes alive in the polluted water.

Studies of the wood used in Stradivarius violins do show that microbes lodged in the wood have hollowed out the cells, leaving only their infrastructure. In the hand of Stradivarius, those hollow chambers were transformed from worthless empty spaces into resonating cathedrals of sound. Every pull of the bow released a magnificent strain of music. Stradivarius rescued worthless scraps of wood, hopelessly damaged and drifting, and transformed them into objects of beauty.

That's what Christ did for us. Broken, abandoned, and lost in the depth of our sin, we were dead in the polluted waters. The hand of the Master Redeemer plucked us out and crafted us into new creations. The hollow cells that sin carved within us now resonate with life sounds that glorify Christ. In turn, we fill our world with the unsurpassed harmony of His presence.

That's why we love Him. That's why we can't stand brooding in the corner with Simon. We belong at His feet with the one who had been forgiven much. Worshiping Him in grateful love and devotion.

Chapter Eight

The good neighbor policy

SO WHO IS MY NEIGHBOR?

Christ knows we love Him by watching what we do with our lives. And how we treat people is the first place He looks.

When a lawyer asked Jesus, "What is the greatest commandment?" Jesus answered by saying that we are to love God with the totality of our being. But what He said next added some definition. Although it was more than the scheming lawyer had asked for, Jesus gave him the second most important command: "Love your neighbor as yourself" (Matthew 22:39). Jesus knew that we can't have one without the other. The Pharisees prided themselves in mastering their love for God, but they were dreadfully lacking in loving their neighbor—which, in Jesus' book, would make the first command null and void.

Jesus underscored that the two commands were inseparably entwined when He spoke of the "second" command. He did not mean the second as inferior to or less important than the first, but rather, second in sequence. The point Jesus was making was this: "If you are gratefully surrendered to Me, then you must love your neighbor." To which we might be tempted to reply, "Lord, you obviously have never met my neighbor! Could we talk about this? I'd be glad to double tithe, send my kids to work in a bug-infested jungle, or even work in the nursery at church!"

He would be unimpressed with the offer. With gentle determination Jesus would remind us that our attitudes and actions toward others prove our love for God.

These two commands are so comprehensive that Jesus said that the *entire Law* stands or falls on them. And that makes sense. If we truly care about our neighbors' welfare, we would never lie to them to gain personal advantage. If we really love someone, we wouldn't covet that person's husband or wife or anything else he or she has. Such sins as adultery and murder would be out of the question if we were focused on the benefit and welfare of our neighbor.

That brings us back to the Pharisees' problem. They felt they fully understood the dynamics of loving God but often debated the issue of who their neighbor really was. In so doing, they argued away most of their responsibility to love others, particularly if the others were the "sinners" in town —the tax collectors, the Samaritans, or for sure, rude cab drivers!

This is why one of the experts in the law who was on the scene asked Jesus, "Who is my neighbor?" Jesus' response is wonderfully instructive and set the stage for Him to tell the story of the Good Samaritan. But before we expose our treatment of others to that story, another key question must be asked. "If I am to love my neighbor as myself, what does it mean to love myself?" If we are clear about this, we will have a clue as to how to love our neighbor.

"WHO IS MY NEIGHBOR?"

Jesus acknowledged that certain aspects of loving ourselves are legitimate. In fact, nowhere in Scripture are we instructed to hate or despise ourselves. Now that is not a license to live selfishly as though we were the most important people in the universe, nor to stop caring for the needs of others. It simply reiterated that some of our instincts are focused inward naturally and productively.

Some time ago I attempted to repair the family hair dryer. As you know, we are all victims of an international conspiracy to build appliances that well-meaning, ordinary husbands can't fix. Determined to beat the system, I went after it anyway. The only way I could reach the screw that was sunk deeply into the plastic cover was to take my old pocketknife and put the skinny blade down the shaft. As I put pressure on the blade in an effort to engage and turn the screw, the pocketknife folded, squeezing my finger against the sharp edge of the blade. I bled like a stuck pig.

My first response was not, "Sorry, I don't have time to take care of you!" Rather, all my attention turned from the important repair job to the need of my finger. I yelled to

Martie, and she came running, with the kids not far behind. She ran some water in the sink to wash the blood off and to stop the bleeding. I begged her not to run the water too cold—or too hot. When the kids pulled out the Band-Aids, I asked that we not cover too many hairs, since I knew it would be torturous to take it off. It was a classic example of self-love—fully attentive, tender, and eager.

That's how I chose to love myself. In essence, our neighbor is to be the recipient of the same favor and grace that we show to ourselves. And the first test of the authenticity of love for Christ is measured by whether we treat others like we'd treat ourselves.

THE GOOD NEIGHBOR

To answer the question "Who is my neighbor?" Jesus told a story about a man attacked on the road leading to Jericho (Luke 10:25–37).

The road from Jerusalem to Jericho was about sixteen miles long, and in that day was considered one of the most dangerous stretches of territory in the region. The terrain provided many rock formations for thieves to hide behind and then flee to for cover. Everyone listening to Jesus knew well the dangers of that winding road.

Jesus said that a man traveling that road fell among thieves, who stripped him of everything, beat him into unconsciousness, and left him for dead by the roadside. Then two prominent, upstanding members of Jewish religious society—a priest and a Levite—came by, the first travelers to see the dying victim.

We are surprised, given our twenty-first-century mindset, that each walked by. We would expect far more of truly religious people. So we usually conclude that they were too busy with appointments and business in Jericho to take the time to stop. For that reason we wag our condemning finger to point out how easy it is for good folk to become messed up in their priorities.

But any Jews listening to the story would understand very well that their system of righteousness *demanded* that these men distance themselves from the traveler. For a priest to come within ten yards of a corpse would have made him ceremonially defiled, which in turn would disqualify him from performing priestly duties for two weeks. Even getting close enough to discern whether the man was dead or alive posed a serious risk to his purity.

Jesus' listeners would assume that the dying man was a Jew, because Jesus said he was traveling from Jerusalem to Jericho. But the priest would not have had a clue. For all the priest knew, the man could be from the enemy territory of Samaria, and that alone would disqualify him as a legitimate object of love. So we can see why the priest actually stayed as far away from the victim as possible. In the priest's mind,

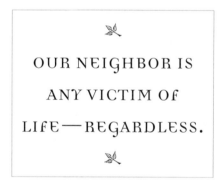

OUR NEIGHBOR IS ANY VICTIM OF LIFE—REGARDLESS.

it was the righteous thing to do—which should give all of us pause about systems of righteousness that blind our hearts and minds to the needs of fellow humans.

The Levite, no doubt having seen how the priest responded, would have excused himself because of the priest's example. Although he was not bound by the same laws of defilement as the priest, the Levite would want to be as proper.

The important dynamic in this story is not that these two men were coldhearted, busy, or insensitive, as we usually conclude. It is rather that *they* were the true victims. They were victims of a view of the law and of righteousness so distorted that it kept them from obeying one of the law's most fundamental commands—to care about the needs of people.

AN UNLIKELY HERO

Then Jesus, the master storyteller, turned the tale in an unexpected direction. He introduced a Samaritan. And what the Samaritan did came as a total surprise to His listeners. If you were Jewish and telling the story instead of Jesus, you might report that the Samaritan saw the victim and finished him off.

The Samaritans and Jews despised each other. Their mutual hatred stretched back for generations. They had ransacked each other's temples. From childhood, the people on both sides were taught to have nothing to do with the other. Who can forget the amazement and shock of the disciples when they saw Jesus speaking with a Samaritan woman (John 4)? So the Samaritan Jesus introduces into the story has all the makings of a real villain.

But Jesus painted the Samaritan as a superhero. He took pity on the victim, cared for him, and provided the means to see him safely restored to health. The actions of the Samaritan stood in bold contrast to the religious Jews, who passed up the opportunity to love for the sake of preserving their perception of the Law.

Christ was defining *neighbor* in a way that extended across religious, ethnic, and class lines. Our neighbor is any victim of life—regardless.

The Samaritan's heroic actions were also noteworthy because Jesus was saying that the most unlikely people—people outside our own religious systems—are often better at loving others than we. Why? Because they are not bound by our prejudices.

Jesus then asked the questioner, "Which of these three do you think was a neighbor to the man who fell into the hands of robbers?" To which the lawyer responded, "The one who had mercy on him." Jesus adds, "Go and do likewise" (Luke 10:36–37).

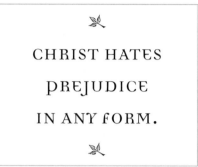

CHRIST HATES PREJUDICE IN ANY FORM.

But the questioner had been interested in who *qualifies* as neighbor. Jesus closed His story with an interesting twist —an emphasis on *who had been neighborly*.

STRUGGLES WITH PREJUDICE

For the average Pharisee, loving his neighbor by this broad definition was out of the question. Their prejudices gave them permission to reduce their circle of involvement to people like themselves. And their prejudices were often supported by self-constructed theology and traditions. Using these as an excuse got them off the hook for caring for the needs of those "other kind" of folk.

For example, the Pharisees had nothing to do with tax collectors. These people were traitors of the worst kind. They had taken jobs with the occupying empire and collected exorbitant taxes. To add insult to injury, they added large assessments and pocketed them. The Pharisees stayed aloof lest they be seen as endorsing these habits.

"Sinners" were in the same league. These were Jews who lived in total disregard of the Law and unabashedly flaunted their lifestyle. You don't have to wonder long why "sinners" did not make the list of those the Pharisees were responsible to love.

Samaritans were politically and religiously abhorrent to these gatekeepers of the true religion.

Women were off the screen as well, since they were viewed not only as chattel by the culture but also as sources of temptation and impurity. Ancient literature records that it was not uncommon for a Pharisee who saw a woman coming down the street to cross to the other side.

Other cultural prejudices were embraced as well. Shepherds, lepers, and beggars were among the untouchables.

That was why the religious leaders were aghast that Jesus spent time with people from these groups. Jesus' ministry demonstrated that *no one* was off His screen and that *prejudice* was not in His vocabulary. He touched lepers. He healed blind beggars. He raised women to their rightful place of honor. He called Himself a shepherd. He ate with tax collectors and sinners. He even led revival meetings in Sychar, the capital of Samaria, after violating prejudicial codes by spending time with a Samaritan woman at the outskirts of town—an immoral woman at that.

Christ hates prejudice in any form. He detests racism, classism, and even religious snobbery. Why? Because they cut across the grain of who He is and what He came to do. Above and beyond everything else, He is a loving God who came to seek and to save those who are lost. He is not, as some like to think, a God who loves only the best of us and hangs out with only the good guys.

Prejudice kills our ability to love without limits and strangles our capacity to love Christ. We cannot love someone we resent or someone we feel distanced from. And if we can't love our "neighbor," we can't love Christ. That is exactly what the apostle John meant when he wrote,

> *If anyone says, "I love God," yet hates his brother, he is a liar.*
> *For anyone who does not love his brother, whom he has seen,*
> *cannot love God, whom he has not seen. And he has given us*
> *this command: Whoever loves God must also love his brother.*
>
> ❧1 John 4:20–21

I can just hear the protests: "Who, me? You've got to be kidding! I don't struggle with prejudice. I'm a new-millennium type of person. You're writing up the wrong tree. After all, didn't we get over all that in the sixties and seventies?"

Well, maybe. But I doubt it. In fact, we as a church may be more in the grip of prejudice today than ever before. We are angry about an awful lot of people, particularly in the light of the political and cultural revolutions we have experienced. We are angry about movies, music, prayer being taken out of the schools and condoms being put in. Opposition to gay liberation and abortion are justifiable concerns, yet they often turn our hearts against the sinners who perpetrate the sin.

What are your feelings toward the doctor who runs the abortion clinic in your town? Have you ever cared for him as a person and prayed that someone would lead him to the Savior? I wonder what our feelings are when we hear news of another abortion clinic practitioner being shot? Is there a sense of "Well, it serves him right"? Or do we weep for his soul?

People who are active in gay agendas often feel little but hate and judgment from "our kind" of people. And it's not that we shouldn't be discerning and clearly articulate our distaste for sin. However, Christ demonstrates the delicate balance between knowing the weight of the sin without forgetting the worth of the sinner.

Not long ago, Matthew Shephard, a gay college student in Montana, was tortured and lynched in one of America's worst hate crimes. The news captured headlines and occupied hours of TV and radio talk shows. Outside the church where his funeral was being held, a minister carried a large placard that read, NO TEARS FOR QUEERS. While few of us would endorse such sub-Christian behavior, that pastor became a media symbol of the attitudes of evangelical Christians. Instead of living compassionate lives, we may be expressing our disdain for sin in ways that give credence to the charge that we hate both the sinner and the sin.

We have spent millions of dollars and phenomenal amounts of time and energy on recapturing America through politics. Yet it hasn't worked. In the wake of the realization that our political companions have betrayed us, we angrily pick up our political toys and leave. And all the while, no one in Washington gets the impression that we care for their souls. It looks as though we were there to use them, not love them.

Think of walking through the mall and seeing a group of "alternative" teens approaching. As they get closer, you notice the arrogant swaggers and hair shaved on one side of the head and styled in red-and-orange spikes on the other. These teens have metal pierced into just about every conceivable place on their bodies, and their wrists are wrapped with leather bands sporting metal spikes.

What is your heart response? Do you pray as you walk by that someone will love them and lead them to Christ? Do you smile at them, hoping to let them know that someone our age really does care? Or does the revulsion in your soul win the day?

Our record with racial issues is not much better. Blatant racism is much subdued today, but we continue to carry prejudicial attitudes in our hearts toward those of different colors and ethnic backgrounds. If we have achieved economic stability, we are tempted to look at people of other races whose lives are in trouble and chalk it up to a lack of initiative. "These people *couldn't* be very good people," we say. "Why don't they get off their fannies, get a job, and live decent lives like the rest of us do!"

If we are part of the majority community we may be especially harsh on people in the minority community. But what do people who have been given the benefit of the doubt at every turn know about the obstacles minorities face and how difficult it is to overcome them?

Many in the minority community may be most like the man dying in the ditch in Jesus' story—true victims. The dynamics that created their living conditions go all the way back to seeds that were planted when their ancestors were torn from their homes and brought to America as slaves. Slavery systematically dismantled the family structure of slaves. It downgraded their sense of worth and dignity. And, worse, slavery was tolerated and even celebrated among many white Christians, even to the point of creating a biblical justification for the inferiority of the black race.

After the liberation of the slaves, blacks were socially

isolated and kept out of the mainstream of privilege and power. Mary McLeod Bethune is heralded today as one of the most outstanding African-American educators in history. She founded a college that still bears her name, and she is commemorated on a recent U.S. postage stamp. What most people don't know is that she came to Moody Bible Institute to become a missionary to her own people in Africa. Yet when she graduated from Moody, not one mission agency would accept her. So she couldn't go.

One of the worst subsidized housing developments in Chicago was planned to be a clustering of poor blacks. A federally funded highway was laid down as a barrier to keep them out of the ethnically powerful neighborhoods on the other side of the freeway. The "projects" that were built cost more than it would have cost to give each of the residents the money to buy his own home!

> ❧
>
> FOR JESUS, THE ISSUE WAS NEVER WHAT THE VICTIM OF SIN SHOULD DO TO HELP HIMSELF.
>
> ❧

Needy people are not always needy because of someone else's sin. But many needy people are. They didn't ask to be born into single-parent homes in the midst of drug- and gang-infested neighborhoods. Because of oppressive cultural systems that are sometimes intentionally put in place, there often is no way out for them. In the pull-yourself-up-by-your-bootstraps type of Christianity, it is easy to say, "Buck up, be good, and get yourself out of there." Or to blame people for the mess they are in without really helping.

I suppose Jesus could have said, "Now, we all know that the man from Jerusalem should not have traveled alone. Really, he should have known that was a horribly dangerous road. And why did he travel without a weapon? If he hadn't been wearing so much gold, those guys may not have been tempted to rob him. You know, don't you, that he always liked to flaunt his wealth. In a way it serves him right. . . ."

But for Jesus, the issue was never what the victim of sin should do to help himself. The issue was giving redemptive love to those in need. That was exactly why Simon could not identify with the love feast at Jesus' feet nor understand the acceptance Jesus showed to an extravagant sinner. In Simon's mind, the woman didn't deserve forgiveness; she needed to stop doing what she was doing. If she would clean herself and her life up, there might be a chance of acceptance.

FINDING YOUR NEIGHBOR

A friend of mine was recently called to the pulpit of a large, influential church in one of America's larger cities. It is a good church that has deep roots in the historical fabric of the city and has a passion to reach its city, as well as the world, for Christ. Part of the package for the senior pastor was a membership at the area's most prestigious golf club.

When my friend learned that the golf club excluded African Americans, he declined the membership. Then a member of the congregation came into his office holding a cube of wood with large nails protruding from it. Hoping to help the new pastor understand that there was good reason not to like minorities, he explained that after the assassination of Dr. Martin Luther King, blacks in that city had thrown the cubes into the streets for people to run over. In response, and at risk to himself and his future at the church, the pastor replied graciously, yet firmly, "You have to understand something: God hates racism, and so do I!"

Several months after arriving in town, my friend struck up a meaningful relationship with a black pastor. Together they are forging a slow but sure path that is breaking down walls that for generations have separated true followers of Christ in that city.

This pastor friend is one of my heroes. His example encourages me to keep my heart clear of the prejudices that prevent me from loving my neighbors—all of them.

> BIBLICAL REPENTANCE DEMANDS THAT WE CHANGE OUR MINDS ABOUT PAST THOUGHT PATTERNS AND THEN, AS A RESULT, CHANGE OUR BEHAVIOR.

Developing a growing love relationship with our Lord requires that we acknowledge who our true neighbors are and repent of the prejudice that has blocked our love for them and for Christ.

Biblical repentance demands that we change our minds about past thought patterns and then, as a result, change our behavior. Although repentance is helped along by feelings of sorrow and remorse, it can be effected simply by acknowledging that something in our life is moving in the wrong direction and then turning our hearts and heads around.

Loving Christ by loving our neighbors involves thoughtful reflection and intentional planning. The target is to develop a spirit of kindness to all who pass our way and mercy to the needy who surround our lives. The lawyer who questioned Jesus had it right. The neighborly one in the story was the one who showed mercy to the mugged man in the ditch. Jesus' response was that those who love their neighbors should go and do likewise.

It is time for reflection. To what kind of neighbors have you not felt much of a responsibility? Is it a matter of prejudice? Bitterness? Ignorance? Business? Apathy? Or have you just never thought of those "others" as neighbors worthy of your love? What plans can you make to extend merciful love in a neighborly way?

Your neighbor is the woman who sits through a green light in front of you, finishing her makeup while you are late for an appointment. It is the man in the "10-items-or-less" line at the grocery store who has seventeen items in his cart. And you know he has seventeen because you counted! Your neighbor is the homeless man sitting in ragged clothes on the park bench.

From your "neighbors" in heavy traffic, to the neighbors next door, to the neighbors in the poorer sections of your town, to the most intimate "neighbors" who live under the same roof, Jesus made one thing crystal clear: Loving Him is about loving them.

Chapter Nine

The ultimate Testimony

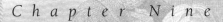

THE COMPELLING
POWER OF A LOVING
COMMUNITY

Philip Yancey opens his book *What's So Amazing About Grace?* with a gripping story that should give all church folk pause. The story is told by a friend who works with the downtrodden in Chicago. It is not unlike the attitudes that filled the dining room at Simon's place.

> A prostitute came to me in wretched straits, home-
> less, sick, unable to buy food for her two-year-old
> daughter. Through sobs and tears, she told me that
> she had been renting out her daughter—two years

> old!—to men interested in kinky sex. She made more renting out her daughter for an hour than she could earn on her own in a whole night. She had to do it, she said, to support her own drug habit. I could hardly bear hearing her sordid story. For one thing, it made me legally liable—I'm required to report cases of child abuse. I had no idea what to say to this woman.
>
> At last I asked if she had ever thought of going to a church for help. I will never forget the look of pure, naïve shock that crossed her face. "Church?" she said. "Why would I ever go there? I was already feeling terrible about myself. They'd just make me feel worse."[1]

Yancey then observed, "What struck me about my friend's story is that women much like this prostitute fled toward Jesus, not away from him. . . . Evidently the down-and-out, who flocked to Jesus when he lived on earth, no longer feel welcome among his followers." In Jesus' day hurting people approached Christ and found refuge, comfort, and forgiveness. Yancey wonders if the church lost the heart of Christ.

LOVE MUST DRIVE AND DEFINE THE WORK AND REPUTATION OF THE CHURCH.

Stories like this shock us. If we look candidly at our churches, we would find too few whose testimony in the community resounds as a place where love prevails. A place known for people who care about each other and about the most despairing.

If that's true, then the church has lost sight of a fundamental command Jesus gave near the end of His ministry as He cast His vision for the church. Jesus said,

> *"A new command I give you: Love one another. As I have loved you, so you must love one another. By this all men will know that you are my disciples, if you love one another."*
>
> ❧John 13:34–35

To fulfill Christ's mandate, love must drive and define the work and reputation of the church. Yet, of all the impressions that the world has of the church, at the bottom of that list are compassion and love. That's a sobering thought.

REACHING NEEDS
THROUGH CHURCH

That was not the case for followers of Christ in the early church. Ostracized and persecuted, first-century Christians were forced to live out Christ's command in dynamic ways. They shared their goods, defended one another in the face of hostile threats, welcomed anyone who would bow the knee to the Master of their souls, and forgave even the worst of sinners and enemies.

Why? Because they loved Christ. They sought to reflect the love He commanded and then demonstrated on the cross. The power of their love for each other and for Christ caught the attention of the pagan world in which they lived. Even the most skeptical among them would say, "See how they love one another."

Historian Will Durant made a relevant and timely observation:

All in all, no more attractive religion has ever been presented to mankind. It offered itself without restrictions to all individuals, classes, and nations; it was not limited to one people, like Judaism, nor to the free-men of one state, like the official cults of Greece and Rome. By making all men heirs of Christ's victory over death, Christianity announced the basic equality of men, and made transiently trivial all differences of earthly degree. To the miserable, maimed, bereaved, disheartened, and humiliated it brought the new virtue of compassion, and an ennobling dignity; it gave them the inspiring figure, story, and ethic of Christ; it brightened their lives with the hope of the coming Kingdom, and of endless happiness beyond the grave. To even the greatest sinners it promised forgiveness, and their full acceptance into the community of the saved. To minds harassed with the insoluble problems of origin and destiny, evil and suffering, it brought a system of divinely revealed doctrine in which the simplest soul could find mental rest. To men and women imprisoned in the prose of poverty and toil it brought the poetry of the sacraments. . . .

>
>
> CHURCH HAS
> BECOME A PLACE
> WHERE MY NEEDS
> ARE MET, MY WAY.
>
>

Into the moral vacuum of a dying paganism, into the coldness of Stoicism and the corruption of Epicureanism, into a world sick of brutality, cruelty, oppression, and sexual chaos, into a pacified empire that seemed no longer to need the masculine virtues of the gods of war, it brought a new morality of brotherhood, kindliness, decency, and peace. So molded to men's wants, the new faith spread with fluid readiness. Nearly every convert, with the ardor of a revolutionary, made himself an office of propaganda.[2]

For many Christians today, church is no longer a place to find Christ's healing love. Many Christians attend church because it's where they grew up or because they think church attendance is the right thing to do. Others come because of inspiring music or appealing worship services. For many, church has become a place to connect, network, and develop a safety net of friends. It has become a place where my needs are met, my way. In fact, if we are not satisfied with what's going on at church, we get grumpy, complain, and eventually leave.

Thankfully, not everyone views church through the lens of satisfying self. Sometime ago I received a letter from an eighty-four-year-old woman who made clear she did not like most of the music we play on the Moody radio stations. But she explained that when she was a teenager, someone ministered to her at her level, and she accepted Christ as her Savior. She said that if young people are being reached for Christ through contemporary music, then she rejoiced. What a refreshing perspective!

Creating an atmosphere of love among believers is a challenge. Churches that take steps to reach out often come under fire for their innovative approaches. Other Christians accuse them of pandering to a consumer mentality. When we understand the Word and are growing spiritually, we can let that love for God outflow in preaching the Word and serving others through practical ministry.

To love Christ means turning away from a self-centered Christianity and focusing on others. It means becoming a community of faith that loves like Christ loves. That translates into real impact.

There are churches meeting the challenge.

One church in the Chicago suburbs connects with people in the community by providing free oil changes and automotive repairs. That may not sound very spiritual, yet this body of believers understood Christ's mission, saw a need in their community, and found an innovative way to meet it. By faith, they believe that simple deeds will open a door for the Gospel. Car maintenance is expensive and requires expertise to carry out correctly, and the church has found a way to give needy people peace of mind about their cars in an unlikely place—the church. I love that!

One group of believers from an affluent community left their comfort zone and planted a ministry on the south side

> THERE IS NO TELLING WHAT CHURCHES FULL OF CHRIST-LOVERS CAN DO WHEN THEY'RE SOLD OUT TO CHRIST.

of Chicago in an area known for high crime and low standards of living. They plan to develop a program in which homeless people are invited to move in with church families. Sound risky? It is. Yet what a picture of Christ's love! They started with an agenda to love like Christ loves. May they never lose their passion!

Because of their outspoken opposition to unrighteousness, Armitage Baptist Church in Chicago has been targeted by radical abortion rights and gay activists. The political extremists want nothing less than to intimidate the church into leaving the community. Weeks before a scheduled demonstration, these groups canvassed the residents of the area, inviting them to join their protest. They were shocked by the response. On the night of the march, not one neighbor could be found. The number of protesters proved embarrassingly small.

I asked the pastor why no one from the community supported the march. He explained that the members of the Armitage Baptist Church had intentionally reached out to the hurting and needy in the community. Many lives were dramatically changed through their compassionate programs. When asked to choose between joining radical extremists and supporting the ministry of the church, the community rallied behind God's people.

I could write an entire book of similar stories of remarkable churches reaching out in love to the most broken communities—each one compelled by the love of Christ.

There is no telling what churches full of Christ-lovers can do when they're sold out to Christ. Think what it would mean to people looking for love if they knew they could find it among the followers of Christ. When loving followers of Christ reflect the glory of their Lord in their community they become like magnets to those with the deepest of needs.

What a privilege we have to extend His love in that way! But you don't have to wait for your church to catch that vision—Christ calls each of us to allow His love to flow through us to those who need it most.

TAKING LOVE PERSONALLY

What does it take to love one another? I love the little song,

To dwell above with saints I loved,
O that will be eternal glory.
To dwell below with saints I know—
That's a different story!

The key to love is found in the roots of Christ's command. When He said this was a *new* command, He meant new in *quality,* not in *time.* There is a sequence here that would have struck a responsive chord in the disciples' minds. In the previous chapter we looked at the two "great" commands: Love God with the totality of your being, and love your neighbor as you love yourself. When Jesus told His disciples to love each other the way He loved them He pointed them to a higher standard.

The new focus is not merely on loving one's neighbors who are outside the church but on loving one's brothers and sisters in Christ. We're to love those called into God's family. Christ told His disciples that their love for one another would demonstrate to the world that they belonged to Him. That's true for us too.

The basis for that new standard of love is Christ's love for us. For three years the disciples enjoyed the blessing of being loved by Christ. They felt His tenderness, kindness, and compassion. They had experienced His sacrificial service. Though the disciples were most times unlovable, Christ loved them in remarkable ways. Let's look at a few of those ways.

Jesus loved the disciples regardless of their temperament problems. That ragtag band of disciples suffered from some serious quirks! Peter had a bad habit of sticking his foot in his mouth. He had to have the last word. He was impulsive. It was Peter who defied the raging storm and leaped out of the boat to go to Jesus. Unpredictable, unreliable, unconvinceable Peter. Yet Jesus loved him just the same.

Then there was Andrew. Although the Bible casts him in the positive light of bringing many to Jesus, he appears to be hardly verbal at all. The only time Andrew is recorded as saying anything is on the occasion of the feeding of the five thousand. Looking for food to feed the crowd, Andrew found a boy who had brown-bagged it to the revival service. The boy's lunch consisted of five loaves and two fish. So Andrew brought the child to Jesus and said, "But what are these among so many?" All day long had Andrew watched Jesus heal the

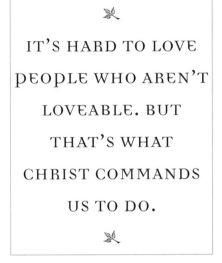

IT'S HARD TO LOVE PEOPLE WHO AREN'T LOVEABLE. BUT THAT'S WHAT CHRIST COMMANDS US TO DO.

sick and give sight to the blind, but it never crossed his fretting mind that the Jesus who could do all that could also supply food for five thousand hungry tourists! Jesus loved Andrew too.

John suffered from a split personality. Though known as the "beloved disciple," he was also known as one of the sons of thunder. The one who wrote so tenderly about the nature of God's love could roar like a summer storm. At one point, he asked Jesus to call down lightning on His enemies. Yet John was the last of the disciples Jesus spoke to before He died.

And of course we can't forget Thomas, the one whose heart was filled with doubt. If you ever want to have a "fun-filled" evening, invite every cynic and skeptic you know to

your party. They will sit around and say, "Oh yeah? Prove it
. . . I told you so." Thomas's heart swelled with doubt until
he came face-to-face with the resurrected Christ. What a
remarkable act of grace for Jesus to offer His wounded
hands to Thomas as proof of His love for him.

Despite their imperfections, Jesus loved those men. If
He could do that, surely you don't have to wait for your
brothers and sisters in Christ to be perfect before you will
allow yourself to love them. Christlike love transcends all
that. It's hard to love people who aren't loveable. But that's
what Christ commands us to do.

Jesus loved His disciples across social and economic barriers.
There is a tendency for individual churches to draw people
from only a small range of social and economic situations.
That's why it's so intimidating to drive a Chevy Cavalier into
a church parking lot lined with Beemers and SUVs! You feel
as though you don't belong there. Christians put up social
and economic barriers all the time—how we dress, the col-
or of our skin, the size of our bank accounts.

The disciples faced the same challenges. James, John,
Peter, and Andrew were fishermen accustomed to working
with their hands. They were tough, independent, and
courageous. Often their trade required that they be out all
night in harsh conditions. They knew the risks but faced
them daily with remarkable courage. It's what they did to
survive. Then there was Matthew. He collected taxes for
Rome. He had a white-collar government job. Probably a
company car and a pension too. No dirt under *his* finger-
nails. He dressed in the finest clothes money could buy.
How different from the fishermen from Galilee.

Simon the Zealot was a ranking member of the anti-
Roman resistance. Now *he* had an agenda! Rome was in his

sights, and he was impatient with Jesus' apparent mission to bring about a peaceful revolution. None of that mattered to Jesus. He loved Simon just the same.

Jesus loved them with His time, talents, and energy. After a busy day of ministry, Jesus got into a boat and told the disciples to take Him to the other side of the lake (Luke 8:22–25). Exhausted, He went to sleep on the floor of the boat. Not long after he had dozed off, a violent storm came up. The disciples were frantic. Convinced the storm meant certain death, they awakened Jesus. He was their only chance at survival. He could have ignored their panicky pleas and drifted back to sleep. But He didn't.

Instead, He felt compassion for them and delivered them from their fear. He got up one more time to love them with His time, talents, and energy. The life-threatening storm disappeared at His command. Only then did He say, "Let me tell you about faith." Loving one another sometimes means that we expend our energy and our talents even when we'd rather be in bed.

> LOVE FOR ONE ANOTHER VALIDATES OUR FAITH TO A JADED AND SKEPTICAL WORLD.

Jesus loved them by laying down His life. The Cross symbolized Christ's supreme act of sacrificial love. John wrote, "This is how we know what love is: Jesus Christ laid down his life for us. And we ought to lay down our lives for our brothers" (1 John 3:16). Christ loved us so that we could love each other. Pretty simple, isn't it? When we follow

Christ's example of love, we're compelled to love others sacrificially. John continued, "Dear children, let us not love with words or tongue but with actions and in truth" (v. 18). He had also offered a specific application. "If anyone has material possessions and sees his brother in need but has no pity on him, how can the love of God be in him?" (v. 17). Christian love demonstrates a genuine desire to meet the needs of others regardless of the cost.

THE DIVERSITY OF LOVE

By loving each other like that we prove we belong to Christ. Love for one another validates our faith to a jaded and skeptical world and allows Christ's love to pour through us into the community.

The prostitute who sold her two-year-old daughter finds a place of refuge in the church. There the body of Christ extends genuine love to this lost woman. That's how a community is transformed: by God's people loving each other and showing that love to others.

In my book *Following Christ* I mentioned that one of my favorite churches is Gospel House, located on the south side of Cleveland. Two men from that fellowship started a ministry to ex-prisoners making the transition back into society. Most churches in the area cared little about these men, but these men, who were sold out to the love of Christ, have made a difference in the lives of hundreds of former criminals.

That's the way it's supposed to work. As the members of Gospel House loved each other, Christ's love spilled out into the community and lives were transformed. The church has flourished. Each Sunday scores of former prisoners and reformed prostitutes worship alongside executives, day laborers, single parents, and large families. What marks this unique ministry? Their love for one another and for their community. A powerful combination!

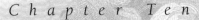

Chapter Ten

street
Love

GIVING THE
DISADVANTAGED
THE ADVANTAGE
OF HIS LOVE

M ichael Brock is a wealthy, upwardly mobile
lawyer. He works for a firm in Washington, D.C. But
he's not real. He is the fictitious hero of John Grisham's
novel *The Street Lawyer,* and his attitude toward the
disadvantaged mirrors that of many Christians.

> The man with rubber boots stepped into the elevator
> behind me, but I didn't see him at first. I smelled him
> though—the pungent odor of smoke and cheap wine
> and life on the street without soap. We were alone as
> we moved upward, and when I finally glanced over I

saw the boots, black and dirty and much too large. A frayed and tattered trench coat fell to his knees. Under it layers of foul clothing bunched around his mid-section, so that he appeared stocky, almost fat. . . . He was black and aging. . . . He didn't belong. It was not his building, not his elevator, not a place he could afford. . . . Just another street bum in from the cold. . . . We had security guards to deal with the riffraff.[1]

We've all been there—revolted by the odor of a homeless man. Thankfully, because of Christ, we don't have to remain like Brock, indifferent to the broken and desperate around us.

But is it enough simply to tolerate the broken and desperate or even to offer them money from time to time? Doesn't Christ call us to love them too? Yes, He does.

When we neglect the neediest among us, we're really neglecting Christ. Most of us live in comfortable environments insulated from the needs of the despairing. We dismiss their troubles as someone else's problem. We may even view these people as irresponsible or threatening. For years, that's how I saw street people. Then we moved to Chicago. Daily I'm confronted with the reality that many of the disadvantaged in American society are true victims with little hope of rescue. Many are buried under the weight of economic and social structures they did not create but keep them in bondage.

We cannot ignore the fact that Christ is deeply interested in what we do to aid the disadvantaged. He sees our activity on this front as a major statement of the authenticity of our love for Him. Read the following verses slowly and prayerfully.

"When the Son of Man comes in his glory, and all the angels with him, he will sit on his throne in heavenly glory. All the nations will be gathered before him, and he will separate the people one from another as a shepherd separates the sheep from the goats. He will put the sheep on his right and the goats on his left.

"Then the King will say to those on his right, 'Come, you who are blessed by my Father; take your inheritance, the kingdom prepared for you since the creation of the world. For I was hungry and you gave me something to eat, I was thirsty and you gave me something to drink, I was a stranger and you invited me in, I needed clothes and you clothed me, I was sick and you looked after me, I was in prison and you came to visit me.'

"Then the righteous will answer him, 'Lord, when did we see you hungry and feed you, or thirsty and give you something to drink? When did we see you a stranger and invite you in, or needing clothes and clothe you? When did we see you sick or in prison and go to visit you?'

"The King will reply, 'I tell you the truth, whatever you did for one of the least of these brothers of mine, you did for me.'"

Matthew 25:31–40

Craig Phillips is an heir to the Wrigley fortune. He was well on his way to wealth and prominence in his own right when he was confronted with the idea of loving Christ by reaching out to the disadvantaged. Since that encounter, he has founded two churches and at the age of eighty-four volunteers at the Wayside Cross Mission in Aurora, Illinois. He writes:

I was working in the Loop as a young 27-year-old and had been gifted with a fine position in one of the Corporate 500 companies. I was walking from the North Shore into the Loop. I walked by the "L" as I would do many mornings, and I'd see people lying in there. One morning I was on the way to my beautiful corporate office with my nice clothes, and my nice tie on and my expensive shoes, and I walked by this alley and saw this broken man lying underneath an elevator where the hot air was coming out for some warmth. Chicago's interesting because on one side is the very elite and right behind it is the very devastating. I walked by, but I couldn't go any further. I turned around and walked back in the alley. I went up to that man and asked, "Is that you, Jesus?" I knew it wasn't Jesus, but I knew that that is where Jesus would be. I said, "Lord, am I on the wrong track looking after material things?" And he said, "Yes, Craig, you are. I told you that a long time ago." And so that's when I changed my goal and went back to what God had touched me as a little boy and said, "Look at the heart, don't look at the outside. God will always reward you."

Since then my life has been a joy because there are so many broken things in life that Jesus can fix. When you let Him do it, you share in that joy. It's greater than any riches you could ever have. It's greater than any material thing. One word with somebody has the power to pick him up and show him Jesus, and let him know that Jesus loves him. No amount of materialism can ever replace that. That lasts for eternity. That's where your treasure is. That's where your heart will be. And no one can take it from you. You can never lose that.

I've always said that if you gain the world, you lose your soul. But if you gain your soul, you don't mind losing the world. People around us are dying. They are waiting. The one in the penthouse, the corporate office, and the one in the alley. They need to know just one thing. He died for them and He loves them. He's not willing that any should perish. He's waiting for them. He's knocking at the door. He's real. He's here. He's in Chicago. He's in your house. He's on your street. He's in your life, and He desires to be in everyone's life. How many times has He wept over Jerusalem, and I think how many times He's weeping over this area, this city of ours, waiting for each one of us to share the Good News. He'll give you that joy when you do. He'll give you that peace. He said it's worth it all. It's worth it all.[2]

After teaching on this topic, I was approached by someone from the audience. He said, "I have trouble getting a grip on loving Christ because I can't see Him or be with Him. But I have found that I can see Jesus in the people I minister to. When I love them, I know that I love Him. It is their presence in my life that brings me close to Him."

That's a great perspective.

FOR I SHALL COME . . .

Leo Tolstoy, the author of *War and Peace,* wrote many short stories, including a lesser-known title, *Where Love Is, God Is.*[3] The story is about a Russian shoemaker, Martin Avdéitch, who lived a hard and disappointing life. His wife died early in their marriage, and his children died in infancy or in early youth. He grew bitter and angry at God, longing for his own death. But in the depths of his despair he met God through the witness of an old man. Christ transformed his life.

As Tolstoy unfolds this story, Martin the shoemaker is reading the account of the sinful woman of Luke 7, as she comes to Simon's house. Martin notes Simon's scandalous treatment of Jesus. Convicted, Martin the shoemaker observed,

"He must have been like me, that Pharisee. He too thought only of himself—how to get a cup of tea, how to keep warm and comfortable; never a thought of his guest. He took care of himself, but for his guest he cared nothing at all. Yet who was the guest? The Lord himself! If he came to me, should I behave like that?"

Then Martin laid his head upon both his arms and, before he was aware of it, he fell asleep.

"Martin!" he suddenly heard a voice, as if someone had breathed the word above his ear.

He started from his sleep. "Who's there?" he asked.

He turned around and looked at the door; no one was there. He called again. Then he heard quite distinctly: "Martin, Martin! Look out into the street tomorrow, for I shall come." . . .

Next morning he rose before daylight, and after saying his prayers he lit the fire and prepared his cabbage soup and buckwheat porridge. Then he lit the samovár, put on his apron, and sat down by the window to his work. As he sat working, Martin thought over what had happened the night before. At times it seemed to him like a dream, and at times he thought that he had really heard the voice. "Such things have happened before now," thought he.

So he sat by the window, looking out into the street more than he worked, and whenever anyone passed in unfamiliar boots he would stoop and look up, so as to see not the feet only but the face of the passer-by as well. A house-porter passed in new felt boots; then a water-carrier. Presently an old soldier of Nicholas' reign came near the window, spade in hand. Martin knew him by his boots, which were shabby old felt ones, galoshed with leather. The old man was called Stepánitch; a neighboring tradesman kept him in his house for charity, and his duty was to help the house-porter. He began to clear away the snow before Martin's window. Martin glanced at him and then went on with his work.

"I must be growing crazy with age," said Martin, laughing at his fancy. "Stepánitch comes to clear away the snow, and I must needs imagine it's Christ coming to visit me. Old dotard that I am!"

Yet after he had made a dozen stitches, he felt drawn to look out of the window again. He saw that Stepánitch had leaned his spade against the wall, and was either resting himself or trying to get warm. The man was old and broken down, and had evidently not enough strength even to clear away the snow. . . .

Martin beckoned to him to come in and went himself to open the door.

"Come in," he said, "and warm yourself a bit. I'm sure you must be cold."

"May God bless you!" Stepánitch answered. "My bones do ache to be sure." He came in, first shaking off the snow, and lest he should leave marks on the floor, he began wiping his feet; but as he did so he tottered and nearly fell.

"Don't trouble to wipe your feet," said Martin. "I'll wipe up the floor—it's all in the day's work. Come, friend, sit down and have some tea."

Filling two tumblers, he passed one to his visitor, and pouring his own out into the saucer, began to blow on it.

Stepánitch emptied his glass, and, turning it upside down, put the remains of his piece of sugar on the top. He began to express his thanks, but it was plain that he would be glad of some more.

"Have another glass," said Martin, refilling the visitor's tumbler and his own. But while he drank his tea, Martin kept looking out into the street.

"Are you expecting any one?" asked the visitor.

"Am I expecting any one? Well, now, I'm ashamed to tell you. It isn't that I really expect any one; but I heard something last night which I can't get out of my mind. Whether it was a vision, or only a fancy, I can't tell. You see, friend, last night I was reading the Gospel, about Christ the Lord, how he suffered, and how he walked on earth. You have heard tell of it, I dare say."

"I have heard tell of it," answered Stepánitch, "but I'm an ignorant man and not able to read."

"Well, you see, I was reading of how he walked on earth. I came to that part, you know, where he went to a Pharisee who did not receive him well. Well, friend, as I read about it, I thought now that man did not receive Christ the Lord with proper honor. Suppose such a thing could happen to such a man as myself, I thought, what would I not do to receive him! But that man gave him no reception at all. Well, friend, as I was thinking of this, I began to doze, and as I dozed I heard some one call me by name. I got up, and thought I heard some one whispering, 'Expect me; I will come tomorrow.' This happened twice over. And to tell you the truth, it sank so into my mind that, though I am ashamed of it myself, I keep on expecting him, the dear Lord!"

Stepánitch shook his head in silence, finished his tumbler, and laid it on its side; but Martin stood it up again and refilled it for him.

"Here, drink another glass, bless you! And I was thinking too, how he walked on earth and despised no one, but went mostly among common folk. He went with plain people, and chose his disciples from among the likes of us, from workmen like us, sinners that we are. 'He who raises himself,' he said, 'shall be humbled and he who humbles himself shall be raised.' 'You call me Lord,' he said, 'and I will wash your feet.' 'He who would be first,' he said, 'let him be the servant of all; because,' he said, 'blessed are the poor, the humble, the meek, and the merciful.'"

Stepánitch forgot his tea. He was an old man easily moved to tears, and as he sat and listened, the tears ran down his cheeks. . . .

"Thank you, Martin Avdéitch," he said, "you have given me food and comfort both for soul and body." . . .

Stepánitch went away; and Martin poured out the last of the tea and drank it up. Then he put away the tea things and sat down to his work, stitching the back seam of a boot. And as he stitched, he kept looking out of the window, waiting for Christ, and thinking about him and his doings. And his head was full of Christ's sayings.

[As Martin worked,] two soldiers went by, one in Government boots and the other in his own. Then the master of a neighboring house, in shining galoshes, passed the house. Then a baker carrying a basket. . . . Then a woman came up in worsted stockings and peasant-made shoes. She passed the window, but stopped by the wall. Martin glanced up at her through the window and saw that she was a stranger, poorly dressed, and with a baby in her arms. . . . The woman had only summer clothes on, and even they were shabby and

worn. Through the window Martin heard the baby crying,
and the woman trying to soothe it, but unable to do so. Martin rose and going out of the door and up the steps he called
to her. . . .

"There, sit down, my dear, near the stove. Warm yourself, and feed the baby."

"Haven't any milk. I have eaten nothing myself since early
morning," said the woman. . . .

Martin shook his head. He brought out a basin and some
bread. Then he opened the oven door and poured some cabbage soup into the basin. . . .

"Haven't you any warmer clothing?" he asked.

"How could I get warm clothing?" said she. "Why, I
pawned my last shawl for sixpence yesterday." . . .

[Martin] looked among some things that were hanging
on the wall and brought back an old cloak.

"Here," he said, "though it's a worn-out old thing, it will
do to wrap him up in."

The woman looked at the cloak, then at the old man, and
taking it, burst into tears. . . .

"The Lord bless you, friend. Surely Christ must have sent
me to your window, else the child would have frozen. It was
mild when I started, but now see how cold it has turned.
Surely it must have been Christ who made you look out of
your window and take pity on me, poor wretch!"

Martin smiled and said, "It is quite true; it was he made
me do it. It was no mere chance made me look out." . . .

"Take this for Christ's sake," said Martin, and gave her sixpence to get her shawl out of pawn. The woman crossed herself, and Martin did the same, and then he saw her out. . . .

After the woman had gone, Martin . . . sat and worked,
but did not forget the window, and every time a shadow fell

on it he looked up at once to see who was passing. People he
knew and strangers passed by, but no one remarkable. . . .

The day wore on, and soon it began to grow dark.

"Seems it's time to light up," thought he. So he trimmed
his lamp, hung it up, and sat down again to work. He finished
off one boot and, turning it about, examined it. It was all
right. Then he gathered his tools together, swept up the cut-
tings, put away the bristles and the thread and the awls, and,
taking down the lamp, placed it on the table. Then he took
the Gospels from the shelf. He meant to open them at the
place he had marked the day before with a bit of morocco, but
the book opened at another place. As Martin opened it, his
yesterday's dream came back to his mind, and no sooner had
he thought of it than he seemed to hear footsteps, as though
someone were moving behind him. Martin turned around,
and it seemed to him as if people were standing in the dark
corner, but he could not make out who they were. And a voice
whispered in his ear: "Martin, Martin, don't you know me?"

"Who is it?" muttered Martin.

"It is I," said the voice. And out of the dark corner
stepped Stepánitch, who smiled and, vanishing like a cloud,
was seen no more.

"It is I," said the voice again. And out of the darkness
stepped the woman with the baby in her arms, and the woman
smiled and the baby laughed, and they too vanished. . . .

And Martin's soul grew glad. He crossed himself, put on
his spectacles, and began reading the Gospel just where it
had opened; and at the top of the page he read, "I was an
hungred, and ye gave me meat: I was thirsty, and ye gave me
drink: I was a stranger, and ye took me in."

And at the bottom of the page he read, "Inasmuch as ye did it unto one of these my brethren even these least, ye did it unto me" (Matt. XXV).

And Martin understood that his dream had come true; and that the Savior had really come to him that day, and he had welcomed him.

Martin Avdéitch understood the power of Christ's love. He had come to the joyful realization that to love those in need was to love his Savior.

ALL THE RIGHT THINGS

You met my dad in a previous chapter. At ninety-two, he has served Christ faithfully for as long as I can remember. During seminary and throughout my ministry, whenever Dad would write he'd end his letters with his life verse: "If you spend yourselves in behalf of the hungry and satisfy the needs of the oppressed, then your light will rise in the darkness, and your night will become like the noonday. The Lord will guide you always; he will satisfy your needs in a sun-scorched land and will strengthen your frame. You will be like a well-watered garden, like a spring whose waters never fail" (Isaiah 58:10–11). Those verses mean more to me now than they ever have in my life.

> IF WE ARE TO LOVE CHRIST WE MUST BE WILLING TO WALK DOWN LIFE'S STREETS WITH HIM.

The passage makes plain what God thinks about the op-pressed and the disadvantaged. He loves them and promises to bless us when we love them too.

Every Christmas afternoon my dad did something that, as a boy consumed with my toys, seemed to me rather strange. As an adult I understand. A few blocks down from our home lived an elderly widow who spent most Christ-mas days alone. Without fail, each Christmas my dad put on his snow boots and coat and trudged through the cold to wish that dear woman a Merry Christmas. I'll never forget that generous deed. I'm sure she didn't either.

My dad not only loved to quote those verses from Isaiah, he lived the truths they taught.

If we are to love Christ we must be willing to walk down life's streets with Him.

One of my favorite experiences at Moody is to be on campus when the new students arrive. I watch as the moth-ers tearfully release their precious cherubs to the wonder and uncertainty of college life. No doubt many feel uneasy about leaving their most prized possessions on Chicago's doorstep.

Yet an amazing thing happens to these students during the years they spend at Moody. They come face-to-face—many of them for the first time—with the lost people of the city. They see what Christ sees, and their hearts break for broken souls. I'm convinced that's why God placed this great school in the heart of a major city. It's because that's where His heart is. And ours should be here too.

Unfortunately, most Christians live their entire lives safely distanced from the pain and suffering of urban life. They never touch people the way Jesus did.

I wonder how Christ feels about churches in the affluent suburbs that remain indifferent to the poor and the disadvantaged. Money flows overseas to lands unknown (and rightly so!) to help people we'll never meet. That's clean and convenient. And that's where we choose to leave it.

Again, I'm culpable too.

One evening as Martie and I were leaving a downtown restaurant following a fabulous steak dinner, a homeless man approached us. He wanted to sell me a copy of a newspaper printed to raise money for people living on the street. But for exact change. All I had was a five dollar bill, which seemed like too much money for a paper. I turned him down flat, to which he replied, "God bless you, brother," and moved on.

The Spirit nailed me instantly! Clutching my doggy bag, I was too full of myself to give five bucks to that desperate man. So I called him back and said that I wanted to give him money in the name of Jesus.

>
>
> WE CAN BECOME CONDUITS OF HIS TRANSFORMING LOVE AND GRACE.
>
>

No sooner had he taken the cash that he asked for my leftovers too!

Fuming, I refused. He thanked me and disappeared. My sense of conviction grew stronger. I felt the weight of my selfishness.

I couldn't believe what I had done. I had just finished writing this chapter. And I missed a perfect opportunity to show Christ's love to someone in need.

Thankfully, Christ offers grace to us in our failure. There's hope for me and for you. We can become conduits of His transforming love and grace.

Unless, of course, we are more taken with our own cash than with Christ.

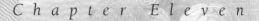

Chapter Eleven

Betrayal

❧

LOVE AT THE
CROSSROADS

Life has a way of pushing us to critical crossroads. Live long enough and eventually you reach the point of needing to decide whether the pursuit of earthly pleasure will be more important than pursuing Christ. Both choices have consequences. For the true disciple to go down the road that leads to material gain forces him to betray Christ.

We all know that's a road well traveled—Jesus called it "the wide road that leads to destruction."

CASH OR CHRIST

Compromising Christ for either cash or comfort puts us in bad company. It may make us uncomfortable to think that we have something in common with the Bible's most famous example of a betrayal—Judas. But embracing that discomfort might help bring the matter into proper perspective. No one wants to be associated with Judas—long considered the worst scoundrel of Scripture. Truth be told, most Christians would discover they have the roots of the same love for self that tempts us to go down that wrong road too.

John 13 paints the backdrop to Judas's betrayal and helps us understand how someone so intimately connected to Christ could become a cold, calculating accomplice to His murder. The chapter takes us to the second-story room in a merchant building in Jerusalem. There Christ was gathered with His disciples to eat their final meal together as a ministry team.

The scene in that upper room is familiar to some believers. That Last Supper has marked the memories of seasoned Christians with images of foot washing, breaking of bread and drinking wine, and Jesus' preparing the disciples for life and ministry without Him. We trace our traditional communion service all the way back to that ominous night before Jesus was betrayed.

Judas dined with Him that night too. He reclined among the rest of the men who had traveled with and served alongside the Master.

What's most remarkable is that most scholars believe Judas held the place of highest honor that night—reclining

immediately left of Jesus. John, the master of understate-
ment, took great care in narrating the details of the evening:

> *It was just before the Passover Feast. Jesus knew that the time*
> *had come for him to leave this world and go to the Father.*
> *Having loved his own who were in the world, he now showed*
> *them the full extent of his love. The evening meal was being*
> *served, and the devil had already prompted Judas Iscariot,*
> *son of Simon, to betray Jesus.*
>
> ❧John 13:1–2

John interrupted the flow of that wonderful thought of
Christ's enduring love by telling us, "The evening meal was
being served, and the devil had already prompted Judas Is-
cariot, son of Simon, to betray Jesus" (v. 2). Judas would
turn against Jesus.

Following the meal, Jesus washed the disciples' feet.
Only Peter resisted because of his pride. What happened
next brought near chaos to that peaceful, tender scene. John
writes:

> *After he had said this, Jesus was troubled in spirit and testified,*
> *"I tell you the truth, one of you is going to betray me."*
> *His disciples stared at one another, at a loss to know*
> *which of them he meant.*
>
> ❧John 13:21–22

The disciples were stunned by what they heard. Their
eyes no doubt darted suspiciously about the room hoping
to catch the villain in a blush.

Unable to contain his anxiety, Peter whispered to John
to pump Jesus for a name. John asked, "Who is it?" Jesus

answered, "It is the one to whom I will give this piece of bread when I have dipped it in the dish" (v. 26). At this point Jesus took some bread and dipped it into a special mixture of raisins, dates, and sour wine—a sauce reserved for feasts such as this. In that Jewish culture, when a host offered you bread dipped in the sop you were considered among the most honored in the room. Jesus not only seated Judas in the place of honor but now affirmed His love for the one who had plotted to betray Him.

> NONE OF US IS
> EXEMPT FROM THE
> DECEITFULNESS
> OF THE HEART.

Judas would betray Jesus—his fate sealed by a morsel of bread.

How could a disciple so intimately related to Jesus, a witness to His miracles, and the object of His deepest affection, do such a thing? What would drive someone who had been so closely associated with Christ for so long to turn on Him so quickly?

Something was wrong with Judas's heart.

MATTERS OF THE HEART

When it comes to betrayal, your external façade is irrelevant, regardless of position, honor, gifts, or capabilities. It doesn't matter whether people look up to you and applaud your achievements. Betraying Christ is always about what's going on in the unseen world of your heart. Whether you betray Him in small or big ways, whether you have a high profile or are unnoticed, it's always the same. It just never becomes obvious until you have first compromised your heart.

None of us is exempt from the deceitfulness of the heart. Some of us have already betrayed Christ in small ways. Others have betrayed Him publicly and shamefully. The externals matter little. What matters is what goes on inside our hearts where no one can see but God. John didn't say, "The devil placed thoughts of betrayal in Judas's *mind*." Satan's target was his *heart*. And he hit it dead center.

BETRAYAL COMES IN
THE FACE OF HIS LOVE

Jesus loved Judas just as He loved the remaining eleven men. He held him in a place of high honor and respect. For three years, Judas had enjoyed the benefits of Christ's generous love and kindness. So how could Judas betray Him? Are you and I capable of a similar betrayal in the face of the abundant love Christ gives us?

Look into His face. He has loved you the way no one has ever loved you. Look at the nail scars in His hands. They are there for your sake. Think of His grace. Look at His daily provision. And what of the mercy He extends to you every day? When we betray Christ, we have to do it in the face of His amazing love for us.

One weekend while Martie cared for one of our grandchildren, I decided to worship at Fellowship Baptist Church —a leading African-American church in Chicago. Pastor Clay Evans founded the church fifty years ago and has become a nationally recognized preacher.

The best part of the service was Dr. Evans's message, based on the passage in John 18 where Pilate, after interrogating

Jesus, comes back out to the crowd and says, "I find no fault in Him." Pastor Evans noted that we live in a world with no-fault divorce and no-fault insurance, yet most of us find fault with just about everything else. He reminded us, through a chorus of "All right," "Don't stop now," and "Well, preacher" responses from the congregation, that there are people who come to church looking to find fault with everything. Then he concluded by saying, "When I see Jesus, I find no fault in Him."

It was a marvelous sermon. As Dr. Evans finished, he reminded the much-involved congregation that if they would take a close look at Christ, they would find no fault in Him as well. It is a wonderful thought. We have and are loved by a no-fault Jesus. If you and I choose to betray Him, we will have to betray Him in the face of His faultless love. He has never given us a reason to betray Him.

BETRAYAL IS STUBBORN

Judas had made the deal to betray Jesus long before that final meal in the upper room. He had been to the religious authorities and negotiated a price. Nothing could deter him from what he had determined in his heart to do. Stubborn Judas.

But why would Judas take that tragic step?

The answer lies in the choices Judas made. Judas's choices over a lifetime brought him to the choice to betray Jesus.

But didn't the Devil make him do it? In a sense, yes. But that's not the whole story. Judas's heart was stubbornly trained to seek after the good of self. He was no pawn in Satan's hand. He willingly participated out of the stubbornness of his heart.

In case we are tempted to think Satan can overcome us against our will, we need to remember what God's Word teaches on that subject. James writes, "But each one is tempted when, by his own evil desire, he is dragged away and enticed. Then, after desire has conceived, it gives birth to sin; and sin, when it is full-grown, gives birth to death (James 1:14–15).

The comedian Flip Wilson used to do a sketch in which his colorful character Geraldine comes home with an expensive new dress. She tries it on for her husband, who immediately asks why she bought it, knowing they had no money for such luxuries. Geraldine

> BEWARE WHEN PEOPLE SOUND TOO SPIRITUAL.

responds, "The Devil made me do it." To which her husband replies, "Why didn't you tell Satan to get behind you?" "I did," Geraldine responds, "and he said it looks good from back here, too."

I love that! Mainly because it explains part of our human nature. We too easily explain away our own sin by pinning it on someone else.

It's hard to love Jesus when your heart stubbornly lobbies for self!

The excuse may have worked for Geraldine's husband, but it won't work with God. We are accountable for all our sin. Our choices cultivate the soil of our hearts to be receptive to the toxic weeds that Satan sows in our lives.

What were the choices that led Judas to betray Jesus? John's gospel gives us clues in chapter 12. The scene is set in the home of Lazarus just after Jesus' miracle of raising

Lazarus from the dead. Needless to say, those were happy days in Bethany, a quiet village just outside Jerusalem. The raising of Lazarus was a truly amazing miracle. Now, because of the loving power of Christ, Mary and Martha had their brother back. Jesus was there along with the disciples. There was rejoicing in the air.

Lost in love and gratitude, Mary, the sister of Lazarus, brought to the feet of Jesus what would have been her most prized possession—a vial of fragrant perfume. Sound familiar? This treasure was worth a year's wages—but that didn't matter to Mary. Her heart overflowed with gratitude for all that Jesus had done. She, like the woman at Simon's banquet, broke the jar and spilled the soothing oil onto Jesus' feet. Judas gasped in disbelief. His heart reeled at the thought of someone wasting something so precious. He growled piously, "Why wasn't this perfume sold and the money given to the poor?"

Beware when people sound too spiritual.

Like Simon in Luke 7, Judas missed the point. He chose to focus on the fleeting value of material things rather than the eternal rewards of sacrificial love. That was only a mild foreshadowing of things to come!

At some point, Judas chose to let his life revolve around money. Cash would rule. He would evaluate everything through dollar signs. His ethics would be dictated by personal gain. That's why he seized the opportunity to betray Jesus for silver.

Once he realized that Jesus had no plans to lead a revolt against Rome, he had to act fast. His dreams of serving as royal treasurer in Christ's newly formed kingdom faded fast with all the talk about death and departure. If Jesus was

headed for the cross, Judas's stealth enterprise had no future. He decided to take the money and run.

LOVE AT THE CROSSROADS

Judas had come to a crossroads. If you had observed Judas at this stage of his life, he would have looked like a
smashing success. You can almost see him sitting at Bennie's
Bistro in some posh neighborhood of Jerusalem, sipping a
latté at the sidewalk café. Maybe he was thinking about the
upcoming weekend, when he'd go to his penthouse over-
looking the Mediterranean. All the while he felt sorry for the
other eleven guys who would be left with nothing but ministry experience. But that's not the rest of the story.

I am reminded of the words of Peter Berger in his book
A Rumor of Angels.

> He who sups with the devil had better have a long spoon, be-
> cause he who sups with the devil will find that his spoon gets
> shorter and shorter until that last supper in which he is left
> alone at the table with no spoon at all and an empty plate.
> But the devil, one may guess, will have by then gone on to
> more interesting company.[1]

Matthew 27 gives us a gripping look at the last chapter
of Judas's life. Long after the deed had been done, Judas,
standing afar off, saw Jesus, hands bound, surrounded by
Roman guards, being led to the trial. Judas had seen those
hands before. He had seen them still the sea and touch the
blind and lame. How often those hands had touched Judas!
An arm around his shoulder. A pat on the back. A wave. A
handshake. A passing of the sop dipped in the rich Passover

sauce. But now Judas saw Jesus' hands bound and his loving leader condemned to die.

Judas's heart swelled with deep, penetrating sorrow. He tried to return the money, but his attempts at assuaging his guilt proved in vain. He ended up throwing the thirty pieces of silver onto the floor of the high priest's chamber. His stubborn heart had won.

When I was a boy, my dad, observing my spendthrift ways, said that money burned a hole in my pocket. Those thirty pieces of silver burned a hole in Judas's heart too, but in a different way. The money made Judas's soul ache. When you and I make choices to betray Christ, sooner or later that betrayal will fill our lives with sorrow. The things we have gained at Christ's expense and the comforts we have enjoyed by resisting sacrifice and suffering for Him will turn to symbols of our sorrow.

Broken and despairing, his scheme came to its logical end. Judas's stubbornness drove him to take his own life.

Betraying Christ may never lead you or me to suicide, but there will be consequences. Francis Schaeffer puts it well in a discussion about 1 Corinthians 3. In that Scripture passage we read that at the end of our lives, we will be led before Christ. All our deeds will be tried by fire. The wood, hay, and stubble of our lives, though not necessarily evil, will be recognized as worthless endeavors that don't count for eternity. The blazing fire of Christ's glory will burn them away. Only those things done for Christ and eternity will remain. They are the gold, silver, and precious stones the text speaks of. We will lay them at Christ's feet in worship and service. On that day, Schaeffer says there will be many "ash heap Christians." When they stand before the Lord, all that they had counted on for eternity will have been burned.

They will be knee-deep in ashes with nothing to present to Him.

We who share space with Judas, who betray Christ for lesser things, will identify with the closing scene of the movie *Schindler's List*. Schindler, who had once been a wealthy businessman, bids farewell to a group of Jews he has delivered from the Holocaust at great personal sacrifice. Suddenly he is gripped with the fact that he's standing by his big, beautiful car. He looks at the car and says, "I could have done more. I should have sold this car. It would have been ten more if I sold this car. This pen—it would have been five more. I could have gotten five more for this pen. This ring—the gold in this ring. I could have gotten two, no maybe one for this ring." The scene closes with him weeping because he could have rescued more people.

I think that when we stand before Christ, even the best of us will say that he could have done more. Knowing this in advance, we should resolve that if Christ pushes against our cash and our comfort, we will choose Christ every time.

So if you have to make a choice between loving cash and comfort and loving Christ, stop for a moment and think of Judas. You may even want to go back and read his story. Then ask yourself this question: *Is it worth it?*

Several years ago on a flight to the West Coast, a young man named Keith approached me and introduced himself. In the course of our conversation, I asked him what he did for a living. Keith said that he was a consultant with a firm that serves the major Fortune 500 companies in the area of strategic planning and corporate training. I told him Moody was looking for a corporate trainer and asked him for his card. I had my doubts that he would want to leave his

Fortune 500 connections for Moody, since there would be no way that we could compete with his salary.

I gave his card to the head of our human resources department. At best, it was a long shot. Keith now heads up our corporate training department. One day when I saw him on our campus I reminded him of our conversation on the plane. I told him I was so thankful that he had come to serve Christ at Moody and thanked him for his sacrifice. I will never forget what Keith said. "It really was not a sacrifice at all. I have always told Christ that He would be first in my life, and now I finally got the opportunity to prove it."

When faced with a crossroads of his own, that young man chose Christ.

I wonder . . . would I? . . . Would you?

Chapter Twelve

After the party

LOVING CHRIST
WHEN LIFE
GOES BACK
TO NORMAL

It would be wonderful to envision living the rest of our lives next to the woman at Jesus' feet. But life rarely permits extended seasons of moving experiences. Good times don't last forever. Life has a way of getting in the face of our well-meaning intentions. Early morning moments with Christ soon give way to the reality of the office and all of its stress and problems. Days are full of the reality of people who make demands on us, disappoint us, manipulate and abuse us, distract and disappoint us. There are spouses who don't share our commitment to a life directed and motivated by love for Christ. There are parents who face the task of refereeing preschoolers and running-nose patrol. Not only do difficulties and discouragement challenge our love for Him, but a myriad of seductions from this world threaten to come between us and an ongoing love-filled life with Christ.

The challenge was no different for our heroine in Luke 7.

> ✿
>
> TRUE LOVERS OF CHRIST RESIST THE TEMPTATION TO RETURN TO LIFE AS USUAL ONCE THEY'VE ENCOUNTERED HIM.
>
> ✿

At some point she, too, had to rise to her feet and make her way through the stunned crowd to return to ordinary living. But once outside Simon's house, she faced the realities of her new life. She could never live the way she once did—and her encounter with Jesus moved her beyond any empty routine of religion. The streets where she once marketed her trade would be the neighborhood where she lived a transformed life as a follower of Christ.

But that transformation held awkward and uncomfortable realities for her. Could she ever live down her reputation? Could she reinvent her life to reflect such radical love? Almost as quickly as she came on the stage, she leaves without a trace. Luke never mentions her again. In fact, we never learn her name. We're left only to ponder her faith and the remarkable deed of love it bore.

So here's a question: Does that sort of passionate love for Christ guide and define your life? If we have been forgiven much, then we, like the woman, must let our love for Christ

permeate our lives. True lovers of Christ resist the temptation to return to life as usual once they've encountered Him.

THE LOOK OF LOVE

If we are not careful, our love for Christ can become
merely another slice of life instead of an all-consuming
reality. You and I face that challenge daily. A genuine love for
Christ should provide the power to transform our response
to everything and everyone in our world. It is a power that
can chase away the lure of lusts, a power able to revolution-
ize our thoughts, fantasies, and dreams. Our love for Christ
should dictate the grid through which we decide how we
use our time, money, and gifts. Nothing should hold back
our expressions of love for Him.

Those who have been forgiven much love Christ with an
all-consuming, all-transforming energy. Christ-lovers never
give in to the notion that Sunday doesn't affect Monday. A
true love for Christ transforms Monday, the workplace, our
homes, our relationships, our addictions, our portfolios,
and our good times and bad.

Is that the kind of life you desire? That's the ultimate
question for all of us.

If you answered yes, the first step toward a life transformed by love is learning to stay in love with Him.

KEEP THE LOVE ALIVE

In elementary school I, along with my buddies, vowed
never to look at, pay attention to, or kiss a girl. That worked
for a couple of years. Then something remarkable happened
in junior high. Girls changed—or was it I? Early experiences

found my heart attracted to a particular girl this week and another the next. I would hear that Alice "liked" me, which would immediately catch my interest. By the time I sent the message back through a network of my friends and hers that I liked her too, she had impatiently moved to someone else. Fickle girls! So I would send word down the line that I liked Barbara, and after a couple of days the word returned that she like me. On it went until . . . well, until Kathy stole my heart.

THE POINT IS TO STAY CONNECTED TO THE VINE.

Christians often adopt the same approach toward Christ. We love Him when we need Him or when we receive His obvious blessing. Yet, in the normal pace of living, He gets crowded out by more attractive alternatives.

Later in my life, I fell in love with Martie. This was serious business now. I began to think that I could—should—marry her. It was time to grow up and learn not only what real love was all about but how to cultivate that love and stay in love—for the rest of my life.

REAL LOVE LASTS

Christ commands us to "remain in my love" (John 15:9). He pictures us as branches intimately connected to Him, the vine. That connectedness guarantees our usefulness and fruitfulness as well as our ultimate fulfillment in life. The point is to stay connected to the vine.

Abiding in Christ means *staying* in love with Him. It is

not temporary, transient, periodic, or based merely on externals. Falling in love and staying in love are often determined by our emotions, experiences, and fulfilled or unfulfilled expectations. C. S. Lewis makes that plain when he writes:

> Being in love is a good thing, but it is not the best thing. It is a noble feeling, but still a feeling. . . . Who could bear to live in this excitement for even five years? But of course, ceasing to "be in love" need not mean ceasing to love. Love in a second sense, love as distinct from being in love, is not merely a feeling. It is a deep unity, maintained by the will and deliberately strengthened by habit; reinforced by the grace which both partners ask and receive from God. They can have this love for each other even at those moments when they do not like each other; as you love yourself even when you do not like yourself. They can retain this love even when each would easily, if they allowed themselves, "be in love" with someone else. "Being in love" first moved you to promise fidelity; this quieter love enables you to keep the promise.[1]

That's the depth of love Christ desires from us.

Being *intentional* about loving Christ is not a one-time decision. We make that decision while we are driving in traffic, or thinking about our coworkers, or judging how we spend our resources. Every life-choice is about staying in love with Christ.

FRUIT IS THE SIGN THAT GENUINE ABIDING HAS TAKEN PLACE.

Abiding in His love is also *reciprocal.* Vines and branches reciprocate in the relationship. The vine is the source of strength, supply, nourishment, and support. The branch bears fruit for the benefit and the glory of the vine. And the branch finds joy and satisfaction in fulfilling its purpose.

Christ teaches us that fruit is the sign that genuine abiding has taken place. When we stay in love with Christ in every choice, action, and attitude, we will be fruitful for Him and a source of blessing to others. For instance, choosing to love Christ by loving those who offend us triggers the fruit of forgiveness. That, in turn, glorifies His character and blesses those who receive forgiveness.

Lest we be tempted to congratulate ourselves, it must be underscored that we do not forgive on our own. We do it for Christ because we love Him more than we hate our enemies. It is what He asks us to do, and He gives us the opportunity to make a statement to Him. Nor can we forgive without having been forgiven by Him first or without having been given the grace to obey. He supplies; we obey. He is glorified and others are blessed. Love makes it all possible— His love for us and our love for Him.

Even the ability to respond to His love must be seen as a gift of His grace. Scripture makes clear that all we do comes by His gracious enablement. The apostle Paul admitted that everything he did came solely by God's grace: "By the grace of God I am what I am, and his grace to me was not without effect. No, I worked harder than all of them—yet not I, but the grace of God that was with me" (1 Corinthians 15:10).

We must rely on God's grace in order to respond lovingly to Jesus. If we could manufacture the capacity to do anything apart from Him, pride would consume our spirit. It is like expressing our love to someone very special with an expensive, well-thought-out gift. After it is given, we feel a need to be recognized for what we have done. It's the old "Who loves ya, baby" need to be praised for the love we have shown. What was intended to be an expression of love ends up being an exercise in self-glorification.

That's why it's so hard to love Jesus. Because to truly love Him we must surrender our love for self. He desires our love and freely enables us to engage it in our hearts. One of my favorite hymns has the line, "O for grace to trust Him more." If I had written the hymn, I would have wanted

> OUR LIVES WOULD NEVER AGAIN BE ORDINARY OR PREDICTABLE.

to sing, "O for grace *to love* Him more." A top priority in our daily prayer must be the heartfelt plea that God will grant us grace to love Him more.

Grace also provides the motivation to love. My constant awareness that I have been forgiven much is a credit to His grace. If it weren't for grace, forgiveness would not be in God's vocabulary. It is the appreciation of His saving grace that gets me up off my knees to search for ways to love Him with an increasing strength. And it is His Word and will that define genuine love for Him.

LIVING LOVINGLY

What would life look like if we were to take up permanent residence in the center of His love?

Our lives would never again be ordinary or predictable.

Authentic love for Jesus has a way of making ordinary people do extraordinary things—like the sinning woman in Luke 7. Christ-lovers do many things the world would consider unusual. We give our money away. We forgive deep and cruel injustices. We see people as more important than material possessions or personal dreams and desires. We ignore barriers of race, class, and culture to embrace the worth of others not like us. We accept and serve other followers of Christ regardless of how we're treated in return. We refuse promotions and job transfers because they conflict with our capacity to serve Him. Ultimately, that love may call on us to give our lives for the sake of His name. Countless Christians through the ages have answered love's ultimate call.

> **WE ARE CALLED TO KEEP OUR FEET ON EARTH AND OUR HEARTS IN HEAVEN.**

I am aware that for many of us to think of suffering as an act of love or to ponder the pain of persecution for Jesus doesn't connect. Yet we must remember that while we are reading these words in the comfort of our well-ordered world, brothers and sisters around the globe risk their lives to love Him. They suffer unbelievable persecution and often death because they refuse to deny His name. In the southern half of Sudan, Christians are executed daily—some crucified, others loaded into trucks to be dumped in the desert to die of starvation. Their children are routinely rounded up to be sold into slavery or prostitution. That's all *before* they're forced to convert to Islam.

Just two weeks ago, a friend of mine who works in Islamic fields told of a friend of his who lived in Khartoum, the capital city of Sudan. His friend watched as a group of several hundred of these children were brought to the city square. The mullah came out of the mosque and commanded that the children bow down and pray a prayer of conversion to Islam. All of the children bowed—except one. He was about nine years old, and when he was asked why he didn't bow down, he simply said he couldn't because he was a child of Jesus Christ. The angry mullah told him to fall down or he would be shot. The child refused, and the mullah ordered the guards to open fire.

As the boy fell to the ground, forty other children stood to their feet in an expression of allegiance to Christ. The mullah ordered four of them shot as well. Frustrated by the resolve of the remaining children, the mullah ordered them taken to prison.

That's a passionate love for Christ!

Any love choice I make for Christ pales into insignificance alongside the courageous love expressed by these young soldiers of the cross. It is hard to complain or wince at the small sacrifices He might demand of me in the light of such moving testimony. Their courageous love is a powerful reminder to you and to me to live out our faith boldly and without complaint, for we "have not yet resisted to the point of shedding your blood" (Hebrews 12:4).

And if all that is not strange enough, Christ-lovers live for another world and can't wait for Him to appear to take them there to be with Him forever. In fact, the Scriptures affirm that a "crown of righteousness" awaits all "who have longed for his appearing" (2 Timothy 4:8). Note that it is a reward for righteous living. When you look forward to your

Lover's return, you live in a state of constant readiness (1 John 3:1–3). The early Christians longed for that day. And so must we. We are called to keep our feet on earth and our hearts in heaven. The Lord wants our love for Him to impact others on earth, and yet, underneath all that, to live with one eye to the sky.

In my book *Eternity* I told the story of the children at the Shepherds Home in Union Grove, Wisconsin. My friend Bud Wood is the founder and developer of what has become one of the finest homes in America for mentally challenged children and adults. Many of the residents of Shepherds Home are afflicted with Down's syndrome. Staff members make a concentrated effort to present Christ's love to all the residents. Many have come to believe in Christ as Savior and in a heaven that will be their home.

Bud told me that one of the major maintenance problems at the home is dirty windows. I had expected him to say fingerprints on walls or mud in the hallways, but I was not ready for what he said next.

"You can walk through our corridors any time of the day," Bud explained, "and see some of these precious children standing with their hands, noses, and faces pressed to the windows, looking up to see if Christ is coming back. They long for the wholeness He promises to bring."

Are you anticipating His return like that?

The children's gaze toward heaven may not seem a normal response from those of us whose lives are more ordinary. But these things are *not* abnormal to us. His love for us and our loving responses to Him are secured by the fact that He works everything together for good for those who love Him (Romans 8:28). Because He loves us, He never wastes our sorrows. Knowing that, we are able to love Him freely and securely without reservation.

When we finally discover that loving Jesus is not hard, but easy, traditions and contrived patterns of religious behavior will no longer stand in love's way.

Unless we, like Simon, forget how much we owe Him.

AFTER ALL HE'S DONE FOR ME

Adolph Hitler was obsessed with eradicating the Jewish race. Their crime? They were born Jewish. To be a Jew in Europe in the 1940s was dangerous and, for most, proved fatal. When the Germans took Denmark, Hitler demanded that all Jewish Danes wear a yellow armband to mark them for deportation to concentration camps. Legend has it that the king of Denmark, Christian X, was forced to read the decree from the balcony of Amalienborg Palace. And then, with tears in his eyes, the king proceeded to put a yellow armband on his arm for all to see. Tradition has it that all the Danish people followed, making it impossible for German troops to tell Jewish citizens from non-Jews.

We have been born sinners. The mark of sin is indelibly printed on us, and our adversary intends to destroy us. And he would—except that the King of Heaven came to live among us. With tears in His eyes, He placed the armband of our sin on Himself and suffered a cruel and unjust punishment in our place. All this so that we might forever be safe from our enemy, eternally hidden in Christ's matchless love.

The sinning woman is one of us. And we are one with her. Though disgraced and judged by Simon the Pharisee, she found an advocate in Jesus—and she found forgiveness.

For this and for all the rest of the abundance of His

grace toward us, how can we help but love Him passionately and eternally!

> *Love so amazing, so divine,*
> *Demands my life, my soul, my all.*

going Deeper

PERSONAL AND GROUP DISCUSSION GUIDE

by Mark Tobey

chapter 1

It's easy to become ensnared by the traps that caught the Pharisees. The four traps are listed again below. Under each one, take some time to reflect on the corresponding questions. It might help to go through these with your spouse, a close friend, or even a small group to ensure a more objective perspective.

Trap #1: *The better we become, the more impressed we are with ourselves.*

In what ways can we become too impressed with our own forms of the Christian life?

What do you think it means to be judgmental? Can you describe a time when you felt looked down upon for a certain attitude or behavior? If so, explain.

In Luke 7, in what ways did Simon demonstrate that he had fallen into this trap? What was the basis for his attitude? How did Jesus know Simon's attitude?

Why does *what we think* have more serious consequences than *what we do or say*? This story demonstrates that Jesus knows and cares deeply about our thoughts. That's because those thoughts betray our attitudes. What attitudes do you have that might not be pleasing to Christ? Do you consider yourself a judgmental person? Why or why not?

Trap #2: *The better we become, the greater distance we place between ourselves and those we consider not as good.*

In what ways do Christians distance themselves from those who are in most need of the Gospel? Can the way Christians in a certain church dress and the cars they drive intimidate less fortunate people from visiting and getting involved?

How diverse is your church? To what extent does your church reflect the community?

In what ways can assumptions distance us from people who have not grown up in church or who haven't had the benefit of good Bible teaching?

Would you be glad if a group of teenagers with nose rings and purple hair started attending your worship service, or would they offend you? Explain.

How many neighborhoods do you drive by or through to get to a church where people seem more like you? Should that matter?

Trap #3: *The better we feel we are becoming, the more godless we may be.*

How would you explain Trap #3 to a group of Christian teenagers?

We talked some about the "fence laws" the Pharisees put in place to keep themselves pure. What sort of fences do you think Christians erect today?

What fence laws have you erected in an attempt to keep you and your family right with God?

What do you feel is the difference between a fence law and a boundary given clearly by God? How do you know the difference? Provide some specific examples.

What segments of society or culture tend to be kept out of mainstream Christianity? How do you feel when a young mother comes to church alone with her several children? In what ways has your church responded to the unique needs of our very complex, broken culture? When you see on the news a report about an individual suffering from *HIV-AIDS* do you feel compassion or disgust? Why?

How do you think Jesus would respond to such desperate needs today?

Trap #4: *The better we become, the more we feel God is impressed.*

What is the danger of thinking that by being good we impress God?

What impressed Jesus the least about Simon? In what ways can our Christian actions impress others but not the Lord?

Though we know God desires we live holy lives, how can our attitudes keep us from expressing genuine love for Him?

Take some time to pray.

Lord Jesus, this has been a hard chapter for me to read. I've seen too much about me that I know dishonors You. In fact, I didn't know that's what this book would be about. Please forgive me for being so impressed with my goodness that I've missed the wonder of Your grace. Help me lovingly and graciously to reach out to someone whom otherwise I might ignore. Help me to stay with this all the way to the end. Because that's what You did for me. Amen.

chapter 2

Take some time and reread Luke 7. Pay close attention to the stories Luke includes about Jesus and the centurion (vv. 1–9) and Jesus raising the widow's son (vv. 11–16). Once you've done that, take some time to reflect on and answer the following questions.

1. Why do you think Luke included the two stories of miraculous healing before he told the story about Simon and the sinning woman? How are the stories the same? How are they different?

2. How did Jesus' growing popularity impact the events of our story? How did the crowd view Jesus and His teaching (v. 29)? What about the Pharisees (v. 30)?

3. Can you describe a time when you felt pressure to be someone you're really not in order to fit in with the crowd? In what ways do you feel tempted to deny Jesus and do what's *acceptable*?

4. Has someone's bold act of love for Jesus ever made you uncomfortable? If so, explain. Do you think it's appropriate for a Christian to become emotional in public about his or her relationship to Jesus? Why or why not? What boundaries exist in your church for what's *appropriate?*

5. How do you express your love for Christ? What keeps you from demonstrating your love for Him boldly?

6. In your worship services, how do you feel when someone lifts hands in praise or waves them in adoration to the Lord? Are you glad or annoyed? Or are you simply uncomfortable? Why?

7. Circle the word(s) below that fits you and your relationship with Christ.

Empty routine   Ritualistic

Off and On   Growing Deeper   Radical

Take some time to pray.

Lord Jesus, some of this hits too close to home. Help me not to close myself to You and Your voice. I need a deeper sense of who I am and how desperately I need You to break through my layers of denial and sin. Don't let go, Lord Jesus, until I'm fully Yours. Amen.

chapter 3

It's possible that as you've read this chapter, you've sensed God speaking to you. Maybe you're feeling convicted about not demonstrating your love for Him in radical response. Or, perhaps your heart has grown more tender . . . and you're beginning to see how much He's really done for you.

I invite you to spend some time with the Lord before moving on to the next chapter. Don't rush past your feelings. God may be speaking to you and long to have some time with you. You can trust Him with your feelings, regardless of how painful they are. Jesus wants to touch you and deliver you from your fears and the pain of your past. He desperately wants to lead you to that place where we find the sinning woman of Luke 7—sitting at the feet of Jesus among those who have been forgiven much. Will you let Him? Will you surrender all the sludge and grime of your past and allow Him to come in?

Take a few moments and write down those things that keep you from trusting Him with everything. Be completely honest. Use the space below to jot down your thoughts.

Take your Bible and read Psalm 139. This is a prayer of David asking God to search the deep, inner places of his heart. Read slowly and prayerfully. As you do, listen for His voice. Don't be afraid of His probing. It may be painful and at times uncomfortable, but if you'll give Him full access to those unattended chambers of your heart, He'll bring light and peace such as you've never known.

If you're serious about really loving Him and moving into an authentic relationship with Him, this is what it will take.

Remember His invitation? *Come to me, all you who are weary and burdened, and I will give you rest. . . .*

Stop fighting your past. Let Him win this one for you. You'll never regret it.

chapter 4

You may be feeling somewhat overwhelmed after reading this chapter. I encourage you to take some time now simply to reflect on what has been said. Don't overanalyze; just think about how you're feeling. As thoughts come to mind, write them down in the space below.

Use your Bible to look up the following verses from the New Testament. For each verse, write down one or two characteristics of God's love and the kind of love He desires from His children.

1 John 2:5

1 John 2:15

1 John 3:1

1 John 3:16, 17

1 John 4:7, 8

1 John 4:16

1 John 4:18–21

In what ways is the love John describes in these verses different than self-love—the love the world promotes?

Why is it so hard to love Jesus out of devotion rather than duty?

In what ways do you feel as though you're going through the motions as you express your love for Christ? What would it take for you to move from being dutiful in your response to Christ to becoming lovingly devoted to Him?

Take some time to pray.

Lord Jesus, help me to see areas in my Christian life where I'm operating out of duty only. Bring back to my heart the thrill and excitement I knew when I first met You. Do whatever it takes to get me past religious activity. And by Your Spirit, show me ways to respond to You with a passionate devotion. I know that's what You desire. Amen.

chapter 5

Tucked away in the Old Testament is a remarkable story about sacrificial love (2 Samuel 24:1–25). Only in this story the main character was no outcast commoner, but God's anointed king. Here David is in the spotlight. After a time of personal and national disobedience, David found himself begging for God's mercy and forgiveness. God's anger had burned against Israel, and He had sent a plague upon the people. God commanded David to build an altar of worship to the Lord as an expression of repentance and humility. When David approached the owner of the field where God intended he build an altar, the landowner begged David to take the land for himself. David replied, "No, I insist on paying you for it. I will not sacrifice to the LORD my God burnt offerings that cost me nothing" (v. 24).

How do you explain David's attitude toward sacrifice?

How is it similar to the attitude we saw in the woman in Simon's house? How is it different?

Of the five qualities of love we've looked at in this chapter, which do you see demonstrated in David's sacrificial act?

Read 1 John 3:18. Why is it so easy to love Jesus with words alone? In what ways can we love Him in our actions?

Why is hard to love Him with our actions?

.

What active expressions of love have you chosen to hold back from the Lord because of the cost involved?

How does this relate to your giving to the Lord? Would you describe yourself as a cheerful giver or one who gives reluctantly when you have a surplus?

Are there habits, temptations, material possessions, or even obsessions in your life that you feel
hinder you from loving Him sacrificially? If so, what
are those things?

What would it take to bring you to a point in
your Christian life where you would willingly live in
full surrender to Jesus?

Like the woman in Luke 7, you may need to
bring those things you treasure most and lay them at
the feet of Christ. Being completely honest with
yourself, make a list of those "tools of your past."
When you're ready, lay them at His feet in prayer.
Then leave them there.

What freedom and release you'll begin to know!

chapter 6

Another individual struggled with a Simonized faith. His name was Peter—the bold, ruddy fisherman who left everything to follow Christ. Yet, in the Gospels we never see a successful Peter. Not until Acts, chapter 2 do we see him transformed into the powerful preacher God used to begin the church.

Read the Scripture passages below and answer the questions that follow.

When Jesus came to the region of Caesarea Philippi, he asked his disciples, "Who do people say the Son of Man is?"

They replied, "Some say John the Baptist; others say Elijah; and still others, Jeremiah or one of the prophets."

"But what about you?" he asked.
"Who do you say I am?"

Simon Peter answered,
"You are the Christ, the Son of the living God."

Jesus replied, "Blessed are you, Simon son of Jonah, for this was not revealed to you by man, but by my Father in heaven. And I tell you that you are Peter, and on this rock I will build my church, and the gates of Hades will not overcome it. I will give you the keys of the kingdom of heaven; whatever you bind on earth will be bound in heaven, and whatever you loose on earth will be loosed in heaven."

Matthew 16:13–19

What do you think is the significance of the question Jesus asked the disciples? Why do you think Jesus wanted to know what people were "saying" about Him?

How do Jesus' follow-up questions differ from His initial one? Why is that significant?

In Matthew 16:6, 11, Jesus warned His disciples to avoid the yeast of the Pharisees. What did He mean? How would you contrast the attitude of the Pharisees and Sadducees at the beginning of Matthew 16 with that of Peter in verse 16? How did Jesus respond to Peter's bold confession?

Not too long after that event Jesus and His disciples approached Jerusalem where He would be falsely charged, subjected to a series of kangaroo trials, and eventually crucified. Read the verses below and answer the questions that follow.

Matthew 26:31–35

How did Jesus' prediction of His death affect Peter? How genuine was Peter's to-the-death allegiance to Jesus? How does it compare to his confession in Matthew 16? How is it different?

Matthew 26:69–75

In what way had Peter misunderstood the cost of loving Jesus to the end?

Why do you think Peter's bold confession in Matthew 16 and his reaffirmation in chapter 26 turned so quickly to denial? In what way can you confess your belief in Jesus yet deny Him openly? Can you describe a time in your life when you did the same?

How did it make you feel? In what ways is Peter's failure similar to Simon's?

Take some time to reflect on your commitment to Christ. Does your confession of Him match your passion for Him today? Don't gloss over these hard questions. Trust God's Word to guide you to those areas you need to repair and bring to Christ.

Lord Jesus, I believe You are who You say You are. Like Peter, I pledge my allegiance to You, no matter what. But, like Simon, I know I'm vulnerable to caring more about religion than about a deep relationship with You. Help me to know the difference between saying, "I love You," and really showing You my love in how I live. Thank You, Lord, for Your unfailing love. Amen.

chapter 7

Only days before Simon's party, Jesus visited Capernaum. While there He encountered a Roman official, whom Luke referred to as a centurion. His story unfolds in Luke 7:1–9.

Here was a man endowed with the authority of the Roman Empire. Yet he approached Jesus on behalf of his servant who was terminally ill. An envoy of Jewish leaders was dispatched on his behalf to summon Jesus. They wanted Jesus to visit the centurion's home and attend to his servant.

Before Jesus arrived, the Roman official met Him on the road and spoke some of the most remarkable words in the Bible. "Lord, don't trouble yourself, for I do not deserve to have you come under my roof. That is why I did not even consider myself worthy to come to you. But say the word, and my servant will be healed. For I myself am a man under authority, with soldiers under me. I tell this one, 'Go,' and he goes; and that one, 'Come,' and he comes. I say to my servant, 'Do this,' and he does it."

His humility and faith amazed Jesus! He had not found such humility and faith in all of Israel—that was surprising enough. What amazed Jesus most was that He found both in the heart of a Roman official.

The irony of that event seen against the backdrop of Simon's story was not missed by Luke. He no doubt deliberately placed both stories in close proximity. The two most unlikely people to understand the depth of their need—an immoral woman and a Roman military officer—got it. Simon—the one who knew the Scriptures and pretended to know God—missed it.

You can see why it's hard to love Jesus when you're focused on your own goodness.

Is it possible you've become so focused on your own form of Christianity that you've missed seeing Christ?

If you're sensing God speaking to you right now, put this book down and just listen. There's plenty of time to finish reading. The Bible says that God speaks with a still, small voice. Bow your head and listen. Ask Him to show you areas in your life you're hiding behind a mask of your own goodness. He wants you to know Him intimately, deeply. But He's having a hard time getting past the trappings of your faith. Speak His name—Jesus . . . Jesus . . . Jesus. Then let Him speak. It's time to surrender everything to Him.

chapter 8

It's easy to watch news reports about racial prejudice and act shocked and dismayed. But we've seen in this chapter that spiritual prejudice is more subtle —and often more damaging.

How do prejudicial attitudes limit our ability to love Christ as He's called us to love Him?

Why do you think Jesus chose to make a Samaritan the heroic figure in the story?

Jesus answered what seemed like a simple question: Who is my neighbor? Why do you think He chose to answer it with a story instead of a direct response?

Read the story of the Good Samaritan in Luke 10:25–37. What emotions do you feel in this story? How does this story compare to the story we've been studying in Luke 7?

How would you compare Simon's attitude to the expert in the Law who was attempting to test Jesus in Luke 10?

What sorts of prejudices have their hold on you? If someone asked you who your neighbor was, could you give an honest reply? How much do you know about your neighbors?

In what ways have you demonstrated love for Christ by reaching out to others in need?

Have you ever asked God, "Who is my neighbor?" Would you be open to His reply?

Take some time to pray.

Lord, I know I've not been the most loving neighbor— not only toward those who literally live next door but toward those who need Your love most. Forgive me for wanting to protect myself from uncomfortable situations. Open my eyes to the needs of others and ways I can meet them in Your name. Amen.

chapter 9

Go back through the chapter you've just read and find the Scripture passages discussed. Write down each one as you find it and look it up in your Bible. Take some time to jot down what each verse says about Christ's love for us and our love for one another.

On a separate sheet of paper, for each verse write out a response to these questions: "What does this passage teach me about God's love? What does it teach me about my love for Him? How can I apply it to my own life?"

Take some time to pray.

Dear Jesus, thank You for loving me unconditionally right from the start. Help me to be more loving toward my brothers and sisters in Christ. Show me the ways I've been unloving. Give me a burden to love the unlovable in my community. I know that's what You desire. Amen.

chapter 10

There's a passage in Matthew's Gospel we must look at before we move on in the book—a passage that receives little attention in our self-serving, me-centered religion. Take your Bible and read Matthew 25:31–46 and answer these questions.

Who was Jesus speaking to in this portion of Scripture? What prompted Him to talk about these things?

According to this passage, what is the key to receiving God's blessing in the life to come?

In what ways can Christians reach out to the disadvantaged according to this passage? Do you think Jesus had a deeper meaning in mind? Why or why not?

The final verses of this passage are haunting. What do you think Jesus means when He says, "Whatever you did not do for one of these, you did not do for me"?

Did Jesus mean that Christians will face eternal judgment if we don't reach out to the homeless and needy? What is Christ teaching about the real meaning of *righteousness?* How does that relate to the story of Simon and the sinning woman?

In what ways could you and your church fellowship demonstrate your love for Christ by reaching out to the disadvantaged in your community?

Take some time to pray.

Lord Jesus, I once was lost, helpless, and in need of You. Thank You for reaching out to me in love and grace. Teach me to love the way You love and to touch those whom You would touch. Forgive me for forgetting how much I owe You. I praise You, Lord. Amen.

chapter 11

Take some time to read John 13. Then answer these questions.

1. There are really three stories in this chapter. What three stories can you identify? In what ways are they related? How are they different?

2. Why do you think John chose to place these three stories close to each other in his Gospel?

3. Jesus makes two major predictions in this chapter. What are they, and what do they involve?

4. Try to place yourself in this scene with Jesus, Peter, Judas, and the other disciples. What would you be feeling? How might you have responded when Jesus asked to wash your feet? What would have been your reaction to the two predictions of denial?

5. Based on your relationship with Christ, circle the words that best describe your level of risk for denying Him.

Extremely low risk   Moderate risk

Above average risk   High risk

Explain your response.

In what ways do you feel you consistently deny your love for Christ? When was the last time you openly and humbly acknowledged those shortfalls to Him? Before moving on to the final chapter of this book, bring your anxieties and doubts to Him. Go boldly! He'll meet you there with arms opened wide.

Notes

Chapter 1: The Eclipse of Devotion

1. Oswald Chambers, *My Utmost for His Highest* (Grand Rapids: Discovery House, 1992), June 19.
2. Roy Clements, *Sting in the Tale* (Leicester, U.K.: InterVarsity, 1995), 78–79.
3. A. M. Hunter, *The Gospel According to St. Mark,* Torch Bible Commentary (London: SCM, 1967), 40–41.

Chapter 2: Bold Love

1. James McBride, *The Color of Water: A Black Man's Tribute to His White Mother* (New York: Putnam/Riverhead, 1996), 42–43.
2. Ibid., 165.
3. Ibid., 50.

Chapter 3: Life Among the Forgiven Much

1. James McBride, *The Color of Water: A Black Man's Tribute to His White Mother* (New York: Putnam/Riverhead, 1996), 217.

Chapter 4: Love, the Way It Was Meant to Be
1. Oscar Wilde, *De Profundis* (published posthumously in 1905; quoted in *Encyclopedia of the Self* by Mark Zimmerman), www.authorslibrary.org.

Chapter 6: Simonized Saints
1. Margie Haack, "Journey to the Stake," *World,* 15 March 1997.

Chapter 7: Barriers to Love
1. *Milk and Honey* (newsletter), December 1997, and *Current Thoughts and Trends* (periodical), April 1998, 21.
2. Barbara Ehrenreich, "What a Cute Universe You Have!" *Time,* 25 August 1997.
3. Ibid.
4. Jerome Miller, *The Way of Suffering: A Geography of Crisis* (Washington, D.C.: Georgetown Univ. Press, 1988), 151.

Chapter 9: The Ultimate Testimony
1. Philip Yancey, *What's So Amazing About Grace?* (Grand Rapids: Zondervan, 1997), 11.
2. Will Durant, *Caesar and Christ* (New York: Simon & Schuster, 1944), 602.

Chapter 10: Street Love
1. John Grisham, *The Street Lawyer* (Garden City, N.Y.: Doubleday, 1998), 9–10.
2. Used by permission of Craig Phillips.
3. Leo Tolstoy, *Where Love Is, God Is* (written in 1885; edited in electronic form by Harry Plantinga in 1995), www.qconline.com/online/martin.html.

Chapter 11: Betrayal
1. Peter L. Berger, *A Rumor of Angels: Modern Society and the Rediscovery of the Supernatural* (Garden City, N.Y.: Doubleday Anchor, 1990), 24–25.

Chapter 12: After the Party
1. C. S. Lewis, *The Problem of Pain* (New York: Touchstone, 1996).

Since 1894, Moody Publishers has been dedicated to equip and motivate people to advance the cause of Christ by publishing evangelical Christian literature and other media for all ages, around the world. Because we are a ministry of the Moody Bible Institute of Chicago, a portion of the proceeds from the sale of this book go to train the next generation of Christian leaders.

If we may serve you in any way in your spiritual journey toward understanding Christ and the Christian life, please contact us at www.moodypublishers.com.

"All Scripture is God-breathed and is useful for teaching, rebuking, correcting and training in righteousness, so that the man of God may be thoroughly equipped for every good work."
—2 TIMOTHY 3:16, 17

MOODY
PUBLISHERS

THE NAME YOU CAN TRUST®

Strength for the Journey- Day by Day with Jesus

ISBN: 0-8024-5645-6, Cloth

This compelling passionate daily devotional by Joseph Stowell will help you access God's Word, His totally reliable source for guidance, comfort, confidence, encourage-ment, and strength in an often dark and treacherous world. As a bonus, the entire book of Proverbs is in-cluded, allowing you to read a chapter a day for 31 days.

"In rare moments of our lives we are called to accomplish some-thing for the Lord in which all of what we are comes together in the work. Strength for the Journey *is such a work for Joe Stowell. As a consummate pastor, he counsels and encourages. As a superb Bible teacher, he thoughtfully opens the Word. As a fellow pilgrim, he comes alongside us and helps us find the strength for one more day's journey."*

– Michael Card, award winning musician & author

MOODY
PUBLISHERS
THE NAME YOU CAN TRUST.

1-800-678-6928 www.MoodyPublishers.org

WHY ITS HARD TO LOVE JESUS TEAM

ACQUIRING EDITOR:
Greg Thornton

DEVELOPMENTAL EDITOR:
Mark Tobey

COPY EDITOR:
Anne Scherich

BACK COVER COPY:
Smartt Guys Design

COVER DESIGN:
Smartt Guys Design

INTERIOR DESIGN:
Ragont Design

PRINTING AND BINDING:
Versa Press Inc.

The typeface for the text of this book is
Berkeley